Providence

Statue of Roger Williams, on the burial monument, overlooking Providence, Rhode Island.

Photograph by Richard Quinney.

Providence
The Reconstruction of Social and Moral Order

Richard Quinney

New York and London

PROVIDENCE
The Reconstruction of Social and Moral Order

Longman Inc., New York
Associated companies, branches, and representatives
throughout the world.

Developmental Editor: Nicole Benevento
Cover Design: Dan Serrano
Manufacturing and Production Supervisor: Kris Becker
Composition: A & S Graphics
Printing and Binding: LithoCrafters Inc.

Library of Congress Cataloging in Publication Data

Quinney, Richard.
    Providence, the reconstruction of social and
moral order.

    (Professional book series)
    Includes index.
    1. Sociology, Christian.   2. Socialism,
Christian.   I. Title.
BT738.056   261   79-20423
ISBN 0-582-28143-1

Manufactured in the United States of America
9 8 7 6 5 4 3 2 1

This book will make a traveller of thee,
If by its counsel thou wilt ruled be;
It will direct thee to the Holy Land,
If thou wilt its directions understand.
Yea, it will make the slothful active be,
The blind, also, delightful things to see.
John Bunyan
The Pilgrim's Progress

Contents

Prologue

To alter John Bunyan's lines in his tale of pilgrimage:

When I took my pen in hand
To write about the material of Providence
I did not know that I would make a little book
In such a mode as this; nay, I had undertook
To make another, but soon realized
That this is the one that must be done—
A book about the grace of Providence.

So we have come finally to the pilgrimage, driven by the desire for satisfactions that are not supplied by our world as currently known.

Now in these days the word of God is seldom heard, and visions are not often granted. We are reaching the end of an age; the advanced capitalist society with its highly secular and utilitarian sensibility is coming to an end. The contradictions of the existing social and moral order and the personal and collective struggle are bringing about a new human history. Jeremiah of the Old Testament signaled the exhaustion of the times and its conventional wisdom, a prophecy that is appropriate to our own time.

The wise men shall be put to shame,
They shall be dismayed and taken;
Lo, they have rejected the word of the Lord,
What wisdom is in them? [JEREMIAH 8:9]

A way of understanding and acting in the world is emerging that combines an apprehension of the earthly kingdom and the kingdom of God. We are beginning to recognize that part of us which is spiritual as well as the material basis of our lives. We may become whole once again—as human beings and as a human society.

An understanding of the social and cultural world requires an imagination that exceeds finite daily existence. Following the social theory of Karl Marx, we are provided with an analysis of human history as being achieved through human action. In the philosophical theology of Paul Tillich, appealing to yet anther discourse as well as offering a critique of secular life, we are given the symbols that help us to integrate our spiritual life with our material historical existence. The task at hand is that of uniting these two forms of thought and belief into a framework for both understanding our human history and acting in the fulfillment of our personal and collective being. We place ourselves within the prophetic tradition in which the human predicament is viewed according to the estrangement between existence and essence and the possibility of a unity with that which is vital to human and social life. Provided is an image of finite existence that is tied to an ultimate concern about the infinite and the eternal. In the principle of socialism—with its prophetic voice and religious symbolism—the fundamental questions of material existence and sacred essence are confronted. By integrating into a Marxist material analysis a critical and prophetic theology of culture, we develop an understanding of the world and a way of transcending the contemporary historical condition. The ancient split between the sacred and the secular is overcome in the struggle for a religious socialist culture. Regained is the dimension of depth in our encounter with reality.

There is a time for understanding through prophecy. The language of the secular priest and the mystic gives way to prophetic wisdom. We draw from the instructive letter of Paul to the Corinthians: "Make love your aim, and earnestly desire the spiritual gifts, especially that you may prophesy." When one uses the language of ecstasy, one is talking with God. On the other hand, when we prophesy, we are talking to other human beings, and our words have power to encourage and to build. The language of ecstasy is good for the speaker, but it is prophecy that builds up a community. Suppose, my friends, that when I come to you I use ecstatic language, including the language of science and material analysis. What good shall I do you, unless what I say contains something by way of revelation, of enlightenment, and of prophecy?

In the prophetic voice we speak with love and understanding to our human predicament. Our finite existence is formed in union with the eternal. History and the transcendent become the nature of our essential being in the world.

1
The Theology Of Culture

And having in a sense of God's merciful providence unto me in my distress called the place Providence.

—ROGER WILLIAMS, 1636

The problem is that of getting to the source again. How are we to reconcile spirit and matter? We are beyond the moment when the separation took place, when we, the subjects in the historical process, became the objects of forces beyond our immediate control. Material conditions and self-consciousness divided us into spirit and matter. We are now estranged from the original union with being.

The goal of fulfillment removes us even further from our origin, but it nevertheless and necessarily brings us closer to our possibilities—to the essence that is possible under the conditions we have made. A dialectic—an opposing of forces—has become the nature of our human existence. We attempt a reconciliation by creating the forms that will permit us to bring our material and spiritual world together, creating a culture that allows us to be whole again.

The conditions of our existence provide the setting for the possibilities of creation and fulfillment. Our future, Karl Marx noted, is to be made "under circumstances directly encountered, given and transmitted from the past." [1] We are thus the products of our culture and creators of it. While our daily struggle is one of transforming the existing order, of removing conditions of oppression and making an authentic existence, a new social order will emerge only out of the productive forces and contradictions of the old order. History is made both subjectively and objectively, as the result of conscious struggle *and* as the development of the economic mode of production.

Our destiny, moreover, is directed by the powers of our origin. In Jewish and Christian thinking, as Paul Tillich has reminded us in his recently translated book *The Socialist Decision*, the symbol of *providence* expresses to us "the confidence that what is is not utterly removed from what should be; that in spite of the present lack of fulfillment, being is moving in the direction of fulfillment." [2] The unity of the "is" and the "ought" is thereby expressed in our understanding of providence. Both Marx and Tillich reaffirm for us the prophetic tradition, the belief in providence. Being moves in the direction of that which is demanded.

Tillich further reminds us that in Marx's analysis of capitalist society, the presupposition of providence receives concrete application and is elaborated by means of scientific methods. Capitalism is in the process of being transformed into socialism. The socialist demand is confirmed by our being: "The forces in the proletarian struggle, the revolt of primal humanity in the proletarian against the class situation, drive toward a socialist society. The promise of socialism grows out of the analysis of being itself."[3] It is in the socialist principle, in our recognition of providence, that we integrate the past, present, and future. We form a bond between origin and a transcendence in the goal of socialism.

HUMAN NATURE AND HISTORICAL CONDITIONS

We begin with the desire to understand the conditions of our contemporary historical existence. We are located in the material world, yet, a comprehension of that world and our place in it requires an imagination that exceeds the details of finite daily existence. It is in both philosophy and religion, serving some of the same needs, that our imagination is enhanced. The myths and images of human nature and social life that are explored in philosophy and theology transcend our concrete historical situation.

Every social theory and every theology imply a conception of human nature. Social theories and theologies also assess the ways and the extent to which this human nature is being realized in the contemporary historical context. Marxism begins with the vision of a "species-being," a basic (universal) human nature that is constantly being uncovered through historical action. As human beings, as species-beings, we are consciously creating our lives. As Marx writes, "Conscious activity is the species character of human beings."[4] In productive life, especially in our work, life is creating life.

However, it is in the contemporary historical situation, under capitalism, that our species-being (our basic human nature) is deprived. Under capitalism our work has become alienated; and "just as alienated labour transforms free and self-directed activity into a means, so it transforms the species-life of man into a means of physical existence."[5] An otherwise productive activity is now directed against ourselves; our work no longer belongs to us as producers. When work ceases to fulfill the human need for expression and communication, we no longer realize ourselves through creation. Moreover, the alienation experienced in labor becomes the condition for all areas of life. Ownership and control of life in general have been surrendered to alien hands.[6] The production of life itself under capitalism has become alienated. Our lives as well as our productions are subverted and alienated in the historical context of capitalism.

From the analysis of alienation in contemporary society emerges the

Marxian possibility of a revolution in conditions that will allow people to achieve the full potential of their self-creativity.[7] Since the conditions under which our self-creation takes place in present society are self-defeating, divorcing us from our essential function, it becomes necessary to transform the world. The Marxist critique of the secular political economy incorporates the call as well as the prescription for redemption.

The questionable character of human existence in our time is basic to Tillich's formulations. Tillich's involvement in the New Hegelian and Marxist intellectual circles between the two world wars, as well as his political activism in the socialist movement, places him in a prophetic line that comes from Marx, and beyond Marx, from the Old Testament prophets. In his own existentialism Tillich explored the "profound relationship" between the existence of the individual and the historical-political situation.[8] This relationship is bound by the character of religion under capitalism, accounting ultimately for the meaninglessness and despair of our time.

Tillich thus accepted and utilized Marx's critique of bourgeois society, but went beyond its materialistic and antireligious basis. Tillich was drawn, in his own words, to the existential strain of Marx's thought: "to his struggle against the self-estrangement of man under capitalism, against any theory that merely interprets the world without changing it, against the assumption that knowledge is quite independent of the social situation in which it is sought."[9] For Tillich, as for Marx, economic materialism is a method of historical analysis and not a metaphysics. This does not imply that the "economic" is the sole principle for interpreting history.

> Economic materialism, however, does show the fundamental significance of economic structure and motives for the social and intellectual forms and changes in a historical period. It denies that there can be a history of thought and religion independent of economic factors, and thereby confirms the theological insight, neglected by idealism, that man lives on earth and not in heaven (or, in philosophical terms, that man lives within existence and not in the realm of essence).[10]

Marxism is a necessary method for unmasking the hidden levels of secular reality. Its far-reaching religious and historical implications, however, are to be found in its prophetic elements. Socialism, Tillich observes, "acts in the direction of the messianic fulfillment; it is a messianic activity to which everybody is called."[11]

The problem in pursuing only the materialist method is that it denies the urgency of the very human nature that it seeks to unmask and recover. Such a materialist methodology for Tillich is a false and dogmatic conception of human nature and historical possibility. The urgency of immediate (material) needs actually is often transcended by other, less material needs. We must acknowledge that "even the most pressing needs are colored by their relationship to other needs, by the specific historical situation in which this constellation of factors has come to be.''[12] A strictly materialist conception of human nature and historical conditions, in fact, is merely another manifestation of the corruptness of the capitalist order. A restricted materialist analysis is itself a part of the human predicament in contemporary culture. The spirit of the age not only affects the way we live but also our daily lives, our way of understanding that life.

The methodology for understanding our world as well as our life within it suffers from the particular capitalist spirit that limits reality to the scientific and technical conquest of time and space. As Tillich describes the condition:

> Reality has lost its inner transcendence or, in another metaphor, its transparency for the eternal. The system of finite interrelations which we call the universal has become self-sufficient. It is calculable and manageable and can be improved from the point of view of man's needs and desires. Since the beginnings of the 18th century God has been removed from the power field of man's activities. He has been put alongside the world without permission to interfere with it because every interference would disturb man's technical and business calculations. The result is that God has become superfluous and the universe left to man as its master.[13]

Under capitalism our actual condition is mistakenly regarded as our essential condition. We continue to be the objects of our own history, left to drift without an ultimate end.[14] This truly is the contemporary human predicament.

The need today is to go beyond materialist analysis and a life devoid of the sacred. Marxism provides the theoretical beginning for understanding life in capitalist society. In spite of the materialist focus Marxism continues to receive from intellectuals, it is consistent with Jewish and Christian theology. We are, according to the prophetic Marx, estranged from our essential nature. True human nature, Tillich notes in his reading of Marx, is impossible under the conditions of capitalism; and true humanity can be achieved only in a protest against this estrangement.[15] Not only will human material existence be revitalized but psychic and social life will be revitalized as well.

The orthodox Marxian vision, nevertheless, is solely this-world oriented: human beings are the measure of all things and have become their own gods by assuming responsibility for the conditions of their own existence. Marx insisted that redemption is limited to the secular world. It is this complete lack of the transhistorical element in Marxism that brings it in opposition to theology. Tillich's theology restores religious symbolism to revolutionary life and offers us a glimpse of the infinite quality of human life. The human situation, rather than being completely bound by time, is thereby "elevated into the eternal and the eternal becomes effective in the realm of time."[16] Reconciliation and redemption can be realized only through an apprehension of the eternal.

MARXISM AND THEOLOGY

The basic question asked in both Marxism and existential theology is the relation between existence and essence—between our essential nature and our existential situation. In the theology of Tillich, consistent with the existential Marx, there are three fundamental concepts that characterize the problem of existence and essence:

> First: *Esse qua esse bonum est.* This Latin phrase is a basic dogma of Christianity. It means "Being as being is good," or in the biblical mythological form: God saw everything that he had created, and behold, it was good. The second statement is the universal fall—fall meaning the transition from this essential goodness into existential estrangement from oneself, which happens in every living being and in every time. The third statement refers to the possibility of salvation. We should remember that salvation is derived from *salvus* or *salus* in Latin, which means "healed" or "whole," as opposed to disruptiveness.[17]

These three considerations—essential goodness, existential estrangement, and the possibility of something else through which the cleavage is overcome—necessarily point to the fundamental theological nature of our secular-philosophical condition.

In the secular form of Marxian thought, the separation of existence and essence, of the "is" and the "ought," is the tragic interpretation of social life. Alienation is the product of a special historical situation and can be overcome only through human action. In the secular form, however, various kinds of human suffering persist even after the transformation of capitalism. Tillich calls for an image of finite existence that is tied to a concern about the infinite. Essence, in other words, is not merely a characterization of a possible finite existence, but an absolute beyond the possibility of any specific finite reality. Going further than existential philosophy, to what may be called a theological *essentialism*, Tillich holds out the possibility of knowing (by grace of faith) the ultimate questions and meaning of life.[18] We may know, or at least attend to, an objective essence beyond finite existence when we allow ourselves to consider infinite being in the universe.

Yet it is the prophetic voice in Marx that has drawn us to the questions of theology. A theology is emerging inspired by the prophetic Marx.[19] There is a rediscovery of the eschatological dimension in both Marxism and theology, a new consideration of the transformation of the world and an opening of the future. Marxism and theology are confronting each other in ways that allow us to understand our existence and to consider our essential (infinite) nature. Redemption is not only an historical phenomenon, but also a religious condition to be realized.

The Marxism that has been known to social theorists is a philosophy confined to the secular world, no matter how prophetic the philosophy may be within that world. Although Marx did not write much about religion, his rejection of it is absolutely clear: religion is a fantasy of alienated humanity.[20] Marx had in mind the religion of Prussian Germany, dominated by a dogmatic Lutheranism, but he also had in mind religion in general. However, religion is important for Marx because he considers it a spiritual compensation that is afforded people frustrated at efforts of material betterment.

> Religious suffering is at the same time an expression of real suffering and a protest against real suffering. Religion is the sign of the oppressed creature, the sentiment of a heartless world, and the soul of soulless conditions. It is the opium of the people.[21]

Religion, according to Marx, is an inverted consciousness of the world; it is produced by individuals, society, and the state, rather than itself producing human, social, and political life. Nevertheless, "the criticism of religion is the premise of all criticism."[22] Before any other criticism can take place, the role of religion has to be examined. A critique of religion, therefore, precedes the critique of other alienating forms and provides the model for criticizing all other forms of alienation.

> It is the *task of history*, therefore, once the *other-world of truth* has vanished, to establish the *truth of this world*. The immediate *task of philosophy*, which is the service of history, is to unmask human self-alienation in its *secular form* now that it has been unmasked in its *sacred form*. Thus the criticism of heaven is transformed into the criticism of earth, the *criticism of religion* into the *criticism of law*, and the *criticism of theology* into the *criticism of politics*.[23]

The rest of Marx's life was spent in an analysis and critique of the secular world.[24]

The orthodox Marxist notion that religion is solely the "opium of the people," the tool of the oppressor, cannot be sustained by subsequent historical evidence. In the United States and in other countries the religious left makes important and leading contributions to emancipation movements. Harvey Cox, in a re-evaluation of Marx on religion, notes some of these movements:

> Religious ideas, and persons inspired by religious beliefs, have made a distinctive contribution to the emancipation movements of our time. Gandhi is the clearest example. But there is also the Buddhist resistance to French and

American colonialism in Southeast Asia. There are the energetic anti-colonial nativist churches of Africa, and the late Eduardo Mondlane, the assassinated Christian leader of the Mozambique National Liberation Front. Malcolm X and Martin Luther King were both, in their own ways, very religious men. Dom Helder Cámara, Bishop of Recife and Olinda, is the spokesman and symbol of the nonviolent movement of poor people demanding social change in Brazil. Indeed one exiled Brazilian political leader told me last year that when the present military junta seized control in Brazil, four Catholics were imprisoned for every one Communist. In Latin America, and in many places in the world, the rich and powerful can no longer look to the Church as a servile ally.[25]

Religion continues to speak to human needs—needs that are present before, during, and after the revolution.

Marx, in his own rationalism and antireligious fervor, underestimated the force of religion in shaping revolutionary consciousness and in evoking action. He not only undercalculated its durability, but he also overlooked its "potential for catalyzing political and cultural transformation."[26] Religious consciousness can be an integral part of class struggle in the move against oppression. Religion, Cox observes, is also protest:

At times it focuses, energizes and motivates the fight against the tyrant. It provides transcendent symbols of aspiration and lustrous images for exposing the slick control mechanisms of any society. It perforates the stifling enclosure of the one-dimensional world. It keeps hope alive when all the empirical evidence looks bad. It permits us to spit at mere "facts" and not become slaves to rationality. It allows us to be a little mad.[27]

The question is not whether religion, but whether the particular symbols and culture that it contains for the elimination of alienation, can promote the emancipation of the working class and the oppressed of the world.

The orthodox Marxist critique of religion, we now understand, is not a theological critique but a political one. Marx and his interpreters viewed religion in terms of its debilitating ideology.[28] Despite considerable evidence for the ideological character of religion throughout history, it is wrong to dismiss the revolutionary as well as humane character of religion. Religion is much more than ideology. And whatever the extent of the ideology, the specific content of that ideology may range from reactionary to revolutionary—as in any other system of thought and belief. Other Marxists have, indeed, pointed to the progressive elements of religion. For example, Antonio Gramsci recognized the sacred and organic roots of the socialist movement in Italy; Max Horkheimer distinguished between "good" and "bad" ideology in religion; and Theodor Adorno observed the dialectical relationship between reason and the Christian faith.[29] Our humanity is not exhausted by our capacities for reason alone. Emancipation and redemption are joined in the fullness of our being.

A neo-Marxian critique of religion examines the alienating elements and forces of contemporary religion. There is a new attitude toward religion, seeking to bring religion to life as a liberating force.[30] Religion as a political theology concerned with and acting against oppressions of all kinds adds a new dimension to Marxism as well as to our lives.

Theology—a Marxist theology—has thus come to serve the critical function. As Cox writes: "Given the fact that myths are often misused against people, as radical theologians we should seek first to expose the structure of mystification. We should be dismantling the cultural, educational and politico-economic pyramids that keep us opiated and colonized."[31] Theology provides us with a critique of the existing order and an imagination of what could be. And the "could be" is in terms of our everday possibilities informed and inspired by an ultimate concern. This is a critical theology that has as its purpose both understanding the world and changing it—all according to a reflection on matters and spirits infinite and eternal. It is, as Tillich noted, a criticism that is rational and at the same time prophetic, implying a transcending of essential being— "revealing to reason the inner infinity of being."[32] My objective is to integrate a critical and prophetic theology into a Marxist material analysis of the world.

SOCIALISM AND RELIGION

The contemporary world is caught in what Tillich calls a sacred void, the human predicament on both a spiritual and sociopolitical level. Among the characteristics that contribute to this void are a mode of production that enslaves workers, an analytic rationalism which saps the vital forces of life and transforms everything (including human beings) into an object of calculation and control, the loss of feeling for the bond with nature and the sense of history, the demotion of our world to a mere environment, a secularized humanism that cuts us off from our creative sources, the demonic quality of the political state, and the hopelessness of the future. We all experience the void:

> Little is left of our present civilization which does not indicate to a sensitive mind the presence of this vacuum, this lack of ultimacy and substantial power in language and education, in politics and philosophy, in the development of personalities, in the life of communities. Who of us has never been shocked by this void when he has used traditional or untraditional, secular or religious language to make himself understandable and has not succeeded and has made a vow of silence to himself, only to break it a few hours later? This is symbolic of our whole civilization.[33]

The void is historical, beginning with the emergence of capitalism and the breakdown of religious tradition under the impact of the enlightenment and bourgeois liberalism. "First among the educated classes, then, increasingly in the mass of industrial workers, religion lost its 'immediacy,' it ceased to offer an unquestioned sense of direction and relevance to human living."[34] Philosophies and popular movements have since attempted to restore or rediscover an ultimate meaning of life and a direction for living.

Recognizing the need for a new religious philosophy and unable to accept the traditional and conventional political and religious views, Tillich sought a social and religious philosophy that would take seriously the social and economic situation of contemporary society. He found in socialism the best resources for dealing with the realities and for constructing a new social order. In making the socialist decision, he urged others to enter into the socialist movement to pave the way for a future union of religion and socialist order.

> We stand in a period of dissolution. A new age of unity is arising. Socialism will form its economic and social foundation. And Christianity stands before the task to convey to this development its moral and religious powers and thereby to initiate a great new synthesis of religion and social structure.[35]

Tillich sensed the beginning of a new age in which the old order would give way to a socialist order combined with an awareness of the divine in human life.

The movement known as religious socialism was started in 1919 by several German theologians and philosophers. It was led by Tillich until he was removed from his teaching position by the Nazis and forced to leave Germany in 1933. Religious socialism—as both a religious and political protest movement—attempted to understand and transcend the contemporary historical situation. It was, as Tillich later wrote, "a comprehensive understanding of existence, the form of the theonomy demanded and expected by our present Kairos."[36]

Tillich makes it clear that religious socialism stands fundamentally on the ground of Marx's analysis of capitalist society. This means: (1) It recognizes that the structure of contemporary society is determined by the capitalist economy; (2) It agrees with Marx that within capitalist society there is a necessary opposition between the owners of the means of production and those who are dependent upon these means; (3) Out of the structure of capitalism and its inherent class struggle arises the marked tendency to overcome the form of society on which that structure depends; and (4) Along with Marx, religious socialism sees in the proletariat the place given by fate for resistance to the capitalist structure of society.[37] And beyond Marx, religious socialism "calls the capitalistic system demonic, on the one hand, because of the union of creative and destructive powers present in it; on the other, because of the inevitability of the class struggle independent of subjective morality and piety."[38] The most decisive religious task on behalf of the present society, therefore, is to participate in exposing and combating demonic capitalism. In so doing, the alliance of religious socialism is with the class struggle of the working class.

Religious socialism necessarily rejects the narrow materialist doctrine of Marxism. It radicalizes Marxism "by shedding those elements of Marxism which are derived from bourgeois materialism or idealism."[39] Religious socialism thus seeks a basis that lies beyond the opposition between the materialistic and the idealistic conceptions of human existence and social life. It has a dual starting point: "namely, the *unity of that which is vital and spiritual* in man, and the simultaneous *disruption of that unity* which is the source of the threat to man's being."[40] The meaning of existence must incorporate *both* the material and the spiritual world. With this conception, in the struggle against demonized society and for a meaningful society, religious socialism discerns a necessary expression for the expectation of infinite being.

It is in the *principle* of socialism that this expectation is found. As a principle, "a dynamic concept that contains the possibility of making understandable new and unexpected realizations of a historical origin," socialism stands in a critical relation to reality.[41] It allows us to assess our situation and to transcend it in terms that are yet to be developed. The socialist principle is not a general demand standing over history, but neither is it merely the description of a unique historical phenomenon.

> Rather it is a particular principle that at the same time expresses human being in general. It is rooted in a primordial human element: the demand, the transcendent, the expectation of the new. This is its universality. It has been formed historically in the development of the Judeo-Christian tradition, down to the Christian humanism of bourgeois society; and it has come to specific realization in the Western proletariat. The Universal and the particular elements—human being (Sein) and proletarian existence (Dasein)—therefore do not stand alongside each other in an unrelated way. They are related through a history that reaches back to the origins of life, and which leads via Christianity and humanism to socialism.[42]

The universal element of socialism is currently being worked out in the particular historical struggle in capitalist society but will find new expression in yet unperceived form.

Socialism faces a problem in breaking out of its origins in capitalism. This is its inner conflict, between origin and goal. The orthodox (secular) socialist interpretation of human nature and society is bound by its origins in a bourgeois humanism which cuts us off from the transcendent. Human life, accordingly, it to be realized only in ourselves; the meaning of life is to be found in a conditional, finite fulfillment. Even in the collectivity of social life, we are left to face our loneliness and emptiness as autonomous beings necessarily separated from the spiritual side of our being. Religion, if allowed into the scheme of things, is merely a private matter, not an integral part of the community. The strategy is misplaced: "To make religion a private matter means to exclude it from the arena of political struggles, and to turn it over to the individual or to a free association of individuals."[43]

Secular socialism is another symptom of the failure of the spirit of bourgeois, humanistic capitalism. A religious socialism, in contrast, understands human life and society in terms of the vital and spiritual center of our being. The basic error of secular socialism is the objectified interpretation of the world that characterizes the capitalist principle in general. Our fulfillment requires more: "The human soul is so constructed as to require a religion, a doctrine about the meaning and center of life."[44] To regain the center of meaning is the objective in the reconstruction of social and normal life.

Hence, it is in the religious dimension of socialism that Tillich sees the hope and possibility of truly transforming human society. There must be an ultimate concern about being, a place for the unconditional in our thought and action. This is to replace the void in contemporary socialism, a void based on a narrowly constructed scientific and technical, deterministic and antireligious, orthodox Marxism. Without a genuinely religious and transcendent dimension, only an earthly and this-worldy fulfillment can be hoped for sometime in the future; and even that is in certain danger of being coopted in the struggle against capitalism when pursued without the element of the spiritual. If a despiritualized socialism is ever established, "without the acceptance of a religious foundation and the symbols expressing it no system of a planned society can escape a speedy self-destruction."[45] A religious socialist society, if it were achieved, would be one in which the class struggle had been replaced not only by a classless society, but also by a social unity (a "sacramental community") in which human activity has meaning in an ultimate as well as temporal sense.

Our transformation would thus transcend the finitudes of the spirit of capitalism; this is the socialist expectation. The prophetic attitude is essential to religious socialism: "Both prophetic and socialist expectation are a protest of life against false concepts of transcendence that inevitably call forth, in opposition, false concepts of immanence."[46] Here is an eschatology working through history but shattering and changing it.

The bourgeois principle is thereby overcome in the interest of a prophetic, socialist faith—according to the expectation embodied in the socialist principle. "The socialist principle makes it possible," Tillich observes, "for socialism to understand itself in terms of its own roots, and that means, religiously, and on the basis of its own prophetic element to take up a relationship again with the prophetic elements in the history of Western religion."[47] The end of socialism's striving transcends the utopian forms that secular socialism assumes under the domination of the bourgeois principle. Religious socialism seeks to penetrate and purify the socialist belief.

The socialist struggle, therefore, requires categories and symbols that speak to the fundamental question of both material existence and sacred essence. Marxism provides a language for the former (material existence) and a conception of the possibilities of a secular, humanistic essence. It also includes the prophetic notion of redemption through a this-worldly socialist society. Marxism, however, fails to provide us with the symbols that relate to questions of the infinite and eternal that we apprehend in our lives. The socialist principle has to address the fullness of our being, responding to our most fundamental needs (spiritual as well as material). Religious symbolism is necessary in all aspects of social and cultural life, in revolution as well as in everyday living. These symbols, Tillich notes, reveal to us what is otherwise unrecognized:

> They open up a level of reality, which otherwise is not opened at all, which is hidden. We can call this the depth dimension of reality itself, the dimension of reality which is the ground of every other dimension and every other depth, and which therefore, is not one level beside the others but is the fundamental level, the level below all other levels, the level of being itself, or the ultimate power of being. Religious symbols open up the experience of the dimension of this depth in the human soul.[48]

Religious symbols relate our lives to the ultimate ground of being.

The ultimate reality, following Tillich, is in the realm of the holy. Religious symbols are symbols of the holy; they are taken from everything which the experienced reality gives us, "because everything that is in the world we encounter rests on the ultimate ground of being."[49] For Tillich the symbol for that ultimate being is the "unconditioned" or the "unconditional," that which transcends the temporal-spatial, the conditioned order of existence. It surpasses every possible conception of concrete being, even a Supreme Being, "transcending any fixation of the divine as an object."[50] The unconditional is the symbol of our ultimate concern.

When we speak of religion and the necessity of the religious dimension in socialism (the dimension which is already present in the socialist principle), we mean religion in the most basic sense of the word—as *ultimate concern*. This is the definition of religion held by Tillich: "The fundamental concept of religion is the state of being grasped by an ultimate concern, by an infinite interest, by something one takes unconditionally seriously."[51] Religion is therefore the substance, the ground, and the depth of human spiritual life. It is the infinite desire to express ultimate meaning in our lives and in the universe.

The socialist expectation is for the time filled with unconditioned meaning in a meaningful social order. That moment of time is signified by the *Kairos*, the prophetic realized through the principle of socialism.

Kairos is the fulfilled moment of time in which the present and the future, the holy that is given and the holy that is demanded meet, and from whose concrete tensions the new creation proceeds in which sacred import is realized in necessary form. Prophetism is consciousness of Kairos in the sense of the words: "Repent; the time (*kairos*) is fulfilled and the kingdom of God is at hand." Thus the sacramental and the critical attitudes are united in the consciousness of the Kairos, in the spirit of prophetism.[52]

The new being—the redeeming creative power in reality—appears at the moment of the reunion of spirit and matter. It effects reconciliation with the ultimate, the unconditional.

THEOLOGY OF CULTURE

The ultimate—that which is divine—is to be found in the everyday life of human existence and in our human history. In an analysis of history and our own time we search for the signs of providence. In the living of our lives we seek that which has unconditional meaning. Yet our understanding and our being are both within a concrete and historical engagement. Spiritual life and historical praxis are one.[53] Our human history— our present condition—is thus to be understood in relation to the divine. Not only do we know history through an apprehension of the infinite, but we also incorporate that history and a sense of the unconditional into our daily lives.

I am arguing that all historical events have their ultimate significance in a reality that transcends them. In II Corinthians 4:18, Paul writes, "Meanwhile our eyes are fixed, not on the things that are seen, but on the things that are unseen: for what is seen passes away: what is unseen is eternal." Likewise, the culture (including the social and moral order) of any society or collectivity has a significance that transcends it. The ultimate meaning of the substance and form of any culture transcends all the empirical realities of finite existence—although the signs of infinite reality are to be sought in the substance of human forms, and these forms are where the infinite is concretely realized. The forms we create and the substance we give these forms have a profound unity with the spiritual depths of our personal and collective being.

I am following here Tillich's notion of the interpenetration of culture and religion, that "as the substance of culture is religion, so the form of religion is culture."[54] Everything in our culture is in some way an expression of the religious situation. And "every religious act, not only in organized religion, but also in the most ultimate movement of the soul is culturally formed."[55] Culture encompasses all human productions, including politics, economics, and science, as well as art, literature, philosophy, and the patterns of social life. As human, creative production, culture is an expression of the ultimate—an enterprise of infinite importance. Culture and religion are joined historically in the social and moral order of any society.

It is through the sacred element of culture that finite and infinite reality are united; and it is in the arena of everyday social and moral life that the sacredness of culture is manifested. Thus, in our symbolic affairs, there is no real distinction between the sacred and the profane. The culture we create is, in this sense, "supernatural" and has the goal of raising us above nature, assuring us "that in some ways our lives count in the universe more than merely physical things count."[56] We know that we are truly represented in something which exceeds ourselves.

Culture is essentially sacred in seeking the perpetuation and redemption of individual and collective life. In the search for meaning in the universe, culture is the constructed means of transcending the material world. This transcendence moves us not only into a symbolic world (apart from the physical world), but it transports us into the realm of infinite concern. We reach out through culture to what remains beyond definition, to that which is beyond ourselves and our concrete existence. Through culture we participate in the ultimate, in the ground of our essential being. We attend to the infinite and are inspired by the unconditional. As in the words of St. John of the Cross: "Our concept of God, a mere feeble analogue of a reality which overflows it in every direction, can be made explicit only in the judgement: Being is Being, an absolute positing of that which, lying beyond every object, contains in itself the sufficient reason of objects."[57] This is an image of the absolute act of being in its pure actuality.

Culture, in other words, is theological. The "theology of culture," as Tillich called it, recognizes "that in every culture creation—a picture, a system, a law, a political movement (however secular it may appear)—an ultimate concern is expressed, and that it is possible to recognize the unconscious theological character of it."[58] Within every cultural creation (including the substructure of the economic order as well as the superstructure of ideas and social institutions) there is a spiritual expression. Given this concept of the unity of the sacred and the profane, Tillich can observe that "there are no persons, scriptures, communities, institutions, or actions that are holy in themselves, nor are there any that are profane in themselves. The profane can profess the quality of holiness, and the holy does not cease to be profane."[59] The religious substance of culture is manifest in all aspects of human culture; every person is in some way related to the unconditional ground of being. The creation of human culture, let us realize, has within it the touch of divine inspiration.

Yet there is the continuous attempt in contemporary culture to divide the religious and the secular into separate realms. Although our essential nature requires the presence of ultimate concern in all areas of our life, the tendency is to establish a separate realm for the religious. The human predicament is determined by this situation, by an estrangement from our true being. "One could rightly say that the existence of religion as a special realm is the most conspicuous proof of man's fallen state." [60] Nevertheless, beyond the actual predicament, the secular and the sacred are rooted in the larger sense of the word, in the experience of ultimate concern. "To the degree in which this is realized the conflicts between the religious and the secular are overcome, and religion has rediscovered its true place in man's spiritual life, namely, in its depth, out of which it gives substance, ultimate meaning, judgment, and creative courage to all functions of the human spirit." [61]

To the extent that life in capitalist society is divided into separate compartments for religion, on the one hand, and secular pursuit on the other, to that extent people have lost the dimension of depth in their encounter with reality. Capitalism has made impossible the construction of a meaningful cultural existence. Capitalism itself has become the symbol of a "self-sufficient finitude." [62] The end result is the estrangement of our relation to ourselves, to others, and to our ultimate being. Autonomous individuals cut off from their roots and from their nature find little support in a human community. The sacred is unfilling and unfilled in such a world.

The project is to create a theonomous culture, a sacramental community, "a more righteous social order, established in the prophetic spirit." [63] The answer to the human predicament is a salvation achieved through overcoming and healing the disparity between existence and essence. The sacred and secular are integrated into the expectant symbol and reality of socialism. The human predicament produced by capitalism is transcended in the creation of a prophetic, socialist faith. The ancient split between secular wisdom and religious faith is thereby overcome in a religious socialist culture. In socialism's final expectation a new being is created: "a radical transformation of human nature, and in the last instance—since human nature constantly grows out of nature as such—a transformation of nature and its laws." [64] Human existance is redeemed through the grace of providence.

NOTES

1. Karl Marx, *The Eighteenth Brumaire of Louis Bonaparte* (New York: International Publishers, 1963), p. 15.
2. Paul Tillich, *The Socialist Decision*, trans. Franklin Sherman (New York: Harper & Row, 1977), p. 108.
3. Ibid., p. 109.
4. Karl Marx, *Early Writings*, trans. and ed. T. B. Bottomore (New York: McGraw-Hill, 1964), p. 127.
5. Ibid., p. 128. On Marx's materialist conception of species-being, see James M.

Glass, "Marx, Kafka and Jung: The Appearance of Species-being," *Politics and Society*, 2 (Winter, 1972), pp. 255–271.

6. Karl Marx, *The Grundrisse*, ed. David McLellan (New York: Harper & Row, 1971), pp. 132–143.

7. Stanley Aronowitz, "Culture and Politics," *Politics and Society*, 6 (no. 3, 1976), pp. 347–376.

8. James L. Adams, "Introduction," to Paul Tillich, *Political Expectation* (New York: Harper & Row, 1971), pp. ix-x.

9. Paul Tillich, *Theology of Culture*, ed. Robert C. Kimball (New York: Oxford University Press, 1959), p. 109.

10. Paul Tillich, *On the Boundary: An Autobiographical Sketch* (New York: Charles Scribner's Sons, 1966), pp. 87–88.

11. Tillich, *Theology of Culture*, p. 198.

12. Tillich, *The Socialist Decision*, p. 114.

13. Tillich, *Theology of Culture*, pp. 43–44.

14. Yet, as Tillich suggests, we still find ways to live creatively in the contemporary condition: "Some may have the strength to take anxiety and meaninglessness courageously upon themselves and live creatively, expressing the predicament of the most sensitive people in our time in cultural production. . . . The great works of the visual arts, of music, of poetry, of literature, of architecture, of dance, of philosophy, show in their style both the encounter with non-being, and the strength which can stand this encounter and shape it creatively" (Ibid., pp. 46–47).

15. Tillich, *Political Expectation*, pp. 90–91.

16. Ibid., p. 91.

17. Tillich, *Theology of Culture*, pp. 118–119. For a discussion of Tillich's writing on the existential problem, see René Visme Williamson, *Politics and Protestant Theology: An Interpretation of Tillich, Barth, Bonhoffer, and Brunner* (Baton Rouge: Louisiana State University, 1976), pp. 3–36.

18. Tillich's interpretation of existentialism is found, among other places, in *Theology of Culture*, pp. 76–111. Also see Louis C. Midgley, *Politics and Ultimate Concern: The Normative Political Philosophy of Paul Tillich*, (Ph.D. diss., Brown University, 1965), pp. 1–49.

19. See, for example, José Miguez Bonino, *Doing Theology in a Revolutionary Situation* (Philadelphia: Fortress Press, 1975); Gustavo Gutiérrez, *A Theology of Liberation: History, Politics and Salvation*, trans. and ed. Sister Caridad Inda and John Eagleson (Maryknoll, N.Y.: Orbis Books, 1973); and José Miranda, *Marx and the Bible: A Critique of the Philosophy of Oppression*, trans. John Eagleson (Maryknoll, N.Y.: Orbis Books, 1974).

20. For a discussion of Marx on religion, see David McLellan, *Marx Before Marxism* (New York: Harper & Row, 1970), pp. 142–143.

21. Marx, *Early Writings*, pp. 43–44.

22. Ibid., p. 43.

23. Ibid., p. 44.

24. Marx's consistent linking of humanistic criticism with atheism reflects in part his own personal religious alienation—being uprooted from his origins and estranged from the Jewish religion that had been practiced in his family for generations. Marx's father, for occupational and political reasons, joined the Protestant church. Marx found it personally necessary to reject his own religious tradition as well as all religious traditions. This was combined with his political and intellectual involvement in the radical post-Hegelian movement, which began as a theological criticism and became a criticism of the social and political order in general. Yet, in the late 1870s and early 1880s, then seriously

ailing, Marx began reading and taking voluminous notes on the German Reformation and its revolutionary aspects. Likely there was the renewed realization that religion, after all, played a significant part in human history and the transformation of the world. See Saul K. Padover, "Introduction: Marx's Religious Views," in Karl Marx, *On Religion*, ed. and trans. Saul K. Padover (New York: McGraw-Hill, 1974), pp. ix–xxvii.

25. Harvey Cox, *The Seduction of the Spirit: The Use and Misuse of People's Religion* (New York: Simon and Schuster, 1973), pp. 130–131.
26. Ibid., p. 190.
27. Ibid., p. 193.
28. Rudolf J. Siebert, "The New Marxist Conception of Christianity: Hope versus Positivism," *Anglican Theological Review*, 59 (July, 1977), pp. 242–244.
29. Ibid., pp. 250–259.
30. Dom Helder Cámara, "What would St. Thomas Aquinas Do If Faced with Karl Marx?" *New Catholic World*, 220 (May/June, 1977), pp. 108–113; Dorothee Soelle, *Political Theology*, trans. John Shelley (Philadelphia: Fortress Press, 1974).
31. Cox, *The Seduction of the Spirit*, p. 192.
32. Tillich, *The Socialist Decision*, p. 150. Also see Tillich, *Political Expectation*, pp. 12–13.
33. Paul Tillich, *The Protestant Era* (Chicago: University of Chicago Press, 1948), p. 60. See the description in Williamson, *Politics and Protestant Theology*, pp. 27–34.
34. Tillich, *Theology of Culture*, p. 106.
35. Quoted, from the German, in John R. Stumme, "Introduction," Tillich, *The Socialist Decision*, p. xiii.
36. Tillich, *On the Boundary*, p. 81.
37. Tillich, *Political Expectation*, pp. 48–49.
38. Ibid., p. 50.
39. Ibid., p. 46.
40. Ibid., pp. 46–47.
41. Tillich, *The Socialist Decision*, p. 9.
42. Ibid., p. 64.
43. Ibid., p. 80.
44. Eduard Heimann, "Tillich's Doctrine of Religious Socialism," in Charles W. Kegley and Robert W. Bretall (ed.), *The Theology of Paul Tillich* (New York: Macmillan, 1952), p. 318.
45. Paul Tillich, "Man and Society in Religious Socialism," *Christianity and Society*, 8 (Fall, 1943), p. 10. See Midgley, *Politics and Ultimate Concern*, especially pp. 59–63, 101–107.
46. Tillich, *The Socialist Decision*, p. 111.
47. Ibid., p. 146.
48. Tillich, *Theology of Culture*, p. 59.
49. Ibid.
50. Ibid., p. 25. The basic concepts of Tillich's theology are discussed in James Luther Adams, *Paul Tillich's Philosophy of Culture, Science, and Religion* (New York: Harper & Row, 1965), pp. 17–64.
51. Paul Tillich, *Morality and Beyond* (New York: Harper & Row, 1963), p. 30.
52. Tillich, *Political Expectation*, p. 61.
53. Bonino, *Doing Theology in a Revolutionary Situation*, pp. 72–73. Also see Walter Leibrecht, "The Life and Mind of Paul Tillich," in Water Leibrecht (ed.), *Religion and Culture: Essays in Honor of Paul Tillich* (New York: Harper & Row, 1959), pp. 16–17.

54. Paul Tillich, *The Interpretation of History* (New York: Charles Scribner's Sons, 1936), p. 50.
55. Tillich, *Theology of Culture*, p. 42. Regarding the term *religion*, Carl J. Armbruster in *The Vision of Paul Tillich* (New York: Sheed and Ward, 1967) notes that Tillich means two things: "In the narrow or ordinary sense it refers to organized religions and their external trappings such as sacred books, creeds, rituals, priests, sacraments, and so forth. In the broader and more basic sense, religion is faith, the interior state of being grasped by an unconditioned, ultimate concern. Sometimes he intends both meanings under the term 'religion'; at other times, only one, and this is made clear by the context or by an express designation" (p. xviii). The concept of *culture*, on the other hand, includes (as in the German *Kultur*) the wide range of phenomena that social scientists designate by both the terms "social" and "cultural." In reference to Tillich's concept of culture, Hammond writes: "Included in the scope of this concept (which may be rendered loosely as 'civilization') are all material products and modes of production, all social institutions, all patterns of thinking and acting, all artistic creations. Tillich understands all of the products of human culture to be aspects of man's self-creation, which is one of the basic functions of life." Guyton B. Hammond, *The Power of Self-transcendence: An Introduction to the Philosophical Theology of Paul Tillich* (St. Louis, Mo.: Bethany Press, 1966), p. 93.
56. Ernest Becker, *Escape from Evil* (New York: The Free Press, 1975), p. 4.
57. Thomas Merton, *The Seven Storey Mountain* (New York: Doubleday, 1970), p. 212, quoting St. John of the Cross.
58. Tillich, *Theology of Culture*, p. 27.
59. Tillich, *On the Boundary*, p. 71.
60. Tillich, *Theology of Culture*, p. 42.
61. Ibid., p. 9.
62. Paul Tillich, *The Religious Situation* (New York: Meridian Books, 1956), p. 82.
63. Tillich, *On the Boundary*, p. 90.
64. Tillich, *The Socialist Decision*, p. 111.

2
Puritan Theology and Early Capitalism

You have all the while God's work to do and your souls to mind and judgment to prepare for, and you are tiring and vexing yourselves for unnecessary things, as if it were the top of your ambition to be able to say, in hell, that you died rich.
RICHARD BAXTER, *Christian Directory*, 1673

We live our daily lives in the tension and bond between the concrete historical situation and the unconditioned depth of our being. Through the "here and now" of existence we experience an awareness and realization of the sacred. The sacred and secular are thus joined: "History in all its spheres is the arena of salvation, the realm in which the demands of the unconditional are confronted. Salvation occurs in time and through community, in the overcoming of the demonic powers that pervert both personal and social life." [1] In life we come to know that which transcends life.

The sacred—the religious element of our being that is directed toward the unconditional—cannot be separated from the rest of culture. Following the theological tradition articulated by Tillich, all sharp distinctions between the sacred and the secular must be eliminated in a recognition of the common source of both religion and culture. "Religion," Tillich wrote, "is the substance of culture, culture is the expression of religion." [2] Implied here is a dialectical relationship between religion and culture: "Religion, in order to achieve realization, must assume form and become culture; in doing so it is religious in both substance and intention. But culture, even when it is not religious by intention, is religious in substance, for every cultural act contains an unconditional meaning, it depends upon the ground of meaning." [3] Yet when religion becomes cultural reality, it loses some of its depth and relatedness to the unconditional, becoming in various degrees "secularized." However, a new religious awareness may be rediscovered in the dialectic of cultural history because the history of a culture is in a broad sense the history of religion.

The cultural history to which I am referring includes the mode of production and all material products, as well as the social institutions, patterns of thinking and acting, and all artistic creations. Culture, in other words, is not merely the Marxian superstructure, using a spatial metaphor, but is the totality of "base" and superstructure. Although religion is usually considered more directly an element of the superstructure, it is part of a dynamic that shapes the economic base of the culture.

A central proposition of the Marxist analysis of history is that there are deep contradictions and dynamic variations in the relationship of production and the superstructural elements. Moreover, when these forces are considered as the specific activities and relationships of real human beings, "they mean something very much more active, more complicated and more contradictory than the developed metaphorical notion of 'the base' could possibly allow us to realize." [4] When we talk about religion and its relation to culture, we are talking about an interconnected process and not a static condition.

The relation of religion to the basic mode of production is especially important, in the sense of even shaping the substructure, when it is the *intention* of religion to affect human life and influence historical development. And it is, indeed, the intention of religion (that is, life lived with the sense of ultimate concern) to be of consequence to the lives of people and institutions in this world as well as in any other. Religion is a force that is constantly making and remaking culture. As with other human creations, it is from the beginning a practice. [5] Religion continually shapes the conditions of the culture within which it is practiced. Therefore we assume the relationship—dialectical and interdependent in both directions—between culture and religion. Religion is a vital and integral part of human history.

REVELATION AND THE MILLENNIUM

With a sense of the ultimate purpose and destiny of humankind, with an eschatological concern, human events in this world are produced consequentially. That our course shall be revealed by divine guidance is a powerful force in historical development. And that a period of prevailing virtue and great happiness, distinct from the imperfections of present existence, will surely come provides a prophetic vision that moves not only human hearts and minds but the material basis of production. Life is produced and life produces; religion and culture as humanly divine and interacting processes are the motivating forces of history.

In the prophetic religions (namely, Judaism, Christianity, and Islam), revelation is a message communicated by God to those (the prophets) who are open to the "Word of God." The Israelite faith looked back to the first books of the Old Testament for its fundamental revelation of God. In prophecy, the Israelites were brought out of Egypt into the Holy Land. Moses and the prophets were the chosen spokesmen who interpreted God's will and purpose.

Accepting the Hebrew Scriptures as preparatory revelation, Christianity maintains that revelation is brought to fruition in the person of

Jesus Christ, God's own Son and perfect image. The Christian revelation is viewed as occurring primarily in the life, teaching, death, and resurrection of Jesus. In his letters, Paul emphasized the indispensability of missionary preaching in ensuring that God's revelation in Christ be communicated to all nations of the world. As a source of religious knowledge and historical vision, as the disclosure of divine purpose, revelation in the Scripture is a source of our history.

The most powerful religious imagery eventually to be brought to colonial America was derived from the New Testament Book of Revelation. That book, written at the end of the first century A.D. by one identified only as John, servant of Christ, describes a vision of Satan being bound and thrown into the bottomless pit and of Christian martyrs being raised from the dead and reigning with Christ for one thousand years. This is a period known as the millennium, during which the yearning for peace, freedom from evil, and the rule of righteousness upon earth are finally realized through the power of God. Among other things, the millennial image is concerned with the earthly prospects of the human community.

The Book of Revelation initially furnished a message for the concrete problems faced by the early Christians. The Romans demanded loyalty of belief as well as political loyalty to the state. As Christianity spread, obedience to the Roman state was increasingly demanded, and persecution of Christians began in earnest. Writing in exile and choosing loyalty to Christ, John sought to strengthen the resolve of those Christians who might waver in their faith.[6] He answered such inevitable questions as why the evil rulers Domitian and Nero were allowed to reign, and why the believers in Christ were allowed to be persecuted. John assures the Christians that they will ultimately reign with a triumphant Christ. Moreover, the unveiling of future events is related to the battles between God and Satan, the force of good against that of evil. After the triumph of the last battle, the world ends with the Last Judgment. The unfaithful are sentenced to the lake of fire, and those who suffered for Christ go to "a new heaven and a new earth" (Revelation 21:1). The holy city, also called the New Jerusalem, descends from heaven: "and there shall be no night there; and they need no candle, neither light of the sun; for the Lord God giveth them light: and they shall reign for ever and ever" (Revelation 22:5). The book closes with Christ assuring John that the future shall not be kept hidden from the faithful.

The Puritans who came to America from England in the seventeenth century drew heavily from the prophesies of the Bible. The millennial tradition of the Old and New Testament served as their guide in a venture that was filled with its own travail and uncertainty. The Book of Revelation became a basic part of the theology of colonial New England. Study of the prophecies was a major activity of such influential theologians as Cotton Mather, Jonathan Edwards, and Timothy Dwight. Through their writings and preachings, these religious leaders made prophetic thought relevant to a wide range of colonial thought and practice.

Confronted with an ambiguous world, the Puritan theologians and their followers were always on the lookout for tell-tale signs of the times. Edwards wrote that he "had great longings for the advancement of Christ's kingdom in the world;" and that he was "eager to read public newsletters, mainly for that end, to see if I could not find some news favorable to the interest of religion in this world."[7] Fascinated by the drama of a divine plan, Edwards preached a series of thirty sermons for a half year in 1739, tracing the plan all the way from Adam's creation and fall down to the present times and the coming millennium and final judgment. The glorious work of God, foretold in the Scriptures, shall renew the world.

The core of New England theology was an implicit faith in God's intention to establish a new kingdom. With the experience of the Great Awakening, some emphasis was given to the belief that the kingdom would also be an earthly kingdom, without necessarily the supernatural appearance of Christ.[8] God works through human beings and their institutions to regenerate the kingdoms of this world. In the thought and beliefs of such theologians as Jonathan Edwards, the importance of prophetic thinking was that it allowed them to understand human history and present conditions by moving *outside* of this world. By viewing the world from the perspective of God's revelation, they could attend to the trans-historical problems of salvation and redemption. These fundamental religious symbols transcend the concrete kingdoms on earth, but such transcendence provides an unconditional theology for living in this world.

What the millennial Christianity of the seventeenth and eighteenth centuries furnished, then, in conjunction with enlightenment thought, was a new relationship between world transcendence and the creation of a just kingdom in this world. The goal of humanity now was "not to escape from this irremediably evil universe which is itself to disappear in time but rather to achieve a happier state on earth accompanied by a fuller realization of the great hidden goods which the universe must contain within itself."[9] Yet, until its eventual decline, the theology of the New England Puritans continued to hold that the ultimate reality was in the kingdom apart from this world, and that any perfection on earth was to be achieved in reference to that other kingdom. And until the coming of the new heaven and new earth, we are to renew and transfigure the worldly kingdom in the image of the holy city.

That there is a divine redeemer who gives meaning to history has been the message of Christianity since the first century. The Son, Jesus Christ, was sent to this world to reveal to us the presence of the unconditional God. In the stream of historical time, human beings exist for a purpose in this world and for a purpose beyond this world. The Christian view of history finally does not depend on the survival of human, this-worldly, institutions and empires. Indeed, "for Christians, history focused on man's fall from grace, his redemption by Christ's suffering and death, and the last Judgment, when those who had faith would be saved and the rest condemned." [10] There is meaning in history even—and particularly—with the end of temporal life.

We live today with the ambiguity inherent in the Christian theology of history. However secularized, we continue to believe in providence, in a benevolent divine intervention into human affairs by an intelligent being, external to nature but part of it. God not only created the world but also governs it and cares for its welfare, according to a purpose, of which we glimpse the shadows in all our faith and doubt.

THE RELIGIOUS AND ECONOMIC LIFE
OF THE PURITANS

In the revolutionary decades of seventeenth century England, much importance was given to the role of prophecy, especially through interpretation of the Bible. Eschatological prophecy became a major part of the Protestant Reformation in England. The effect of reading the Bible was liberating, as Christopher Hill notes in his study of radical ideas during the English Revolution: "By understanding and cooperating with God's purposes men believed they could escape from the blind forces which seemed to rule their world, from time itself; they could become free." [11] By the mid-seventeenth century the advent of remarkable events seemed imminent with the likely fall of the Antichrist, perhaps the second coming, and the millennium. This provided the basis for the utopian enthusiasm of the Puritan preachers and the call of the common people to fight the Lord's battles against the Antichrist. The Biblical prophecies contained a message of direct contemporary relevance.

As in earlier times, seventeenth century Christianity opened the gates of salvation to all, and "neither wealth nor knowledge nor intellectual prowess counted for anything, but only steadfastness of faith and decency of conduct." [12] In its rites and in its teachings a revitalized Christianity had special attractions for the common poor. During the 1640s and 1650s, laymen (and "mechanick preachers") like John Bunyan interpreted the Bible with the confidence and excitement of a new discovery. For the religious dissenters and for the common people, the Bible was now the accepted source of all true knowledge and faith. The untrained minds of people like Bunyan, Arise Evans, and George Fox were "grappling with the problems of their society, problems which called urgently for solution, and they were using the best tools they knew of." [13]

The relevance of the Bible to contemporary problems was enhanced by its complete accessibility; each person with the spirit of God within could properly understand the Scriptures. In his writings of 1653, entitled *An Eccho to the Voice of Heaven*, Arise Evans wrote: "Afore I looked upon the Scripture as a history of things that passed in other countries, pertaining to other persons; but now I looked upon it as a mystery to be opened at this time, belonging also to us."[14] Within the congregation of believers, interpretations were shared and approved. Each believer thus became a priest and a prophet in his or her own conscience. Without the authoritarian mediation of the rulers of the nation or the priests of the Church, each person in the context of the fellowship of believers was set face to face with God.

Although the doctrine of predestination abstractly set some people apart as an elect, the theory of justification by faith that it inspired gave an inner hope. The theory, in fact, "gave a select group of the unpriviledged third estate sufficient courage, conviction and sense of unity with each other to be able to force their way towards religious and political freedom by means of a tightly disciplined organization."[15] In other words:

> This double sense of power—individual self-confidence and strength through unity—produced that remarkable liberation of energy which is typical of Calvinism and the sects during our period. Men felt free: free from hell, free from priests, free from fear of worldly authorities, free from the blind forces of nature, free from magic. The freedom might be illusory: an inner psychological self-deception. Or it might correspond to outer reality, in that it was likely to be felt by men who were economically independent. But even an illusory freedom might give a man the power to win real freedom.[16]

Certainly there were real social and theological contradictions in sixteenth century Protestantism, but the overall creed was a revolutionary one. As with Luther: "Here I stand, so help me God, I can no other."

For the radical Protestants of the English Revolution there is the belief in the evolution of truth. History is a process towards full revelation of the truth.[17] The revelation is possible to the common people who have received the spirit of God, to those who have the inner grace to understand. Truth is learned in communion with God and one's fellow believers. The poor, the laborers, and the oppressed are free in conscience to engage in revolutionizing their religion, their political forms, and their society. The radical millenarian hope of a new world is here and now as well as there and then. While not all Puritans shared the activism of a John Bunyan, heaven was nevertheless to be striven for. In Bunyan's epic of the itinerant we are told that God will ask at the day of judgment, "Were you doers, or talkers only?"

Among the early Puritans another directive was certain: the admonition against riches. In the last half of the seventeenth century, Richard

Baxter, one of the many English Puritans to write on Puritan ethics, constantly insisted that God and Mammon are antithetical. In particular, the person who seeks riches is "like a foolish traveler, who, having a day's journey to go, doth spend all day in gathering together a load of meat and clothes and money, more than he carry, for fear of wanting by the way."[18] The person who makes private gain the goal, according to early Puritan ethics, denies the end of the religious calling. One must constantly "take heed lest, under the pretense of diligence in your calling, you be drawn to earthly-mindedness, and excessive cares or covetous designs for rising in the world."[19]

Only later, well into the eighteenth century, in the American colonies in particular, did the Puritan admonition against worldly riches become tempered by the new and rising commercialism. When the spirit of capitalism began to gain the upper hand, Puritanism ceased to be Puritanism. As one present-day critic of the thesis that attempts to associate Puritanism with the rise of capitalism observes, "Far from being the logical flowering of certain inherent tendencies in Puritanism, the economic ethics which increasingly dominated English commercial and business life toward the close of the seventeenth century were the very antithesis of those which were fundamental to the whole Puritan outlook."[20] Any acceptance of the capitalist spirit by the Puritans is an illustration of the existential problem faced by any religious movement when confronted with the realities of the prevailing political and economic structure. The rise of capitalism meant the crumbling of the economic foundation upon which early Puritanism rested. As I will argue further in the next section, the development of capitalism in the United States marked the decline of the religious (and anticapitalist) values represented in early Puritanism.

The Puritans that settled in the American colonies were faced with the realities of establishing a new life on the basis of the religious principles that were being formed among the radical Christian sects of England and other parts of Europe. To create a social form that would embody the ideas and ethics of radical Protestantism was the necessary task of the immigrant Puritans. From the beginning, even during their crossing of the waters and amid the chaos of new physical surroundings and rapidly changing economic conditions, these Christian immigrants made a desperate effort to live according to their religion.

The Puritan settlers wished to form a new kind of community dedicated to the principles of their faith. John Winthrop of the Massachusetts Bay colony, drawing from the Scriptures, noted in crossing the Atlantic with fellow Puritans that "We shall find that the God of Israel is among us." Winthrop saw the new colony not as the New Jerusalem itself, which could come only with God's direct intervention in the millennium, but as a precursor of it. The new community, as "a City upon a Hill," would be closely connected to the goals of the religion, informing the political and economic life of its members as well as the religious life.

The New England Puritans thus sought a strong communal tie in fulfilling their religious faith. We have entered "into a covenant," Winthrop told the colony, a community of people bound in a special compact with God and each other. This community, so covenanted, was the unique creation of New England Puritanism.[21] It was the most appropriate form for promoting the shared religious ideals in the course of settling a new world. An uncertain and often hostile environment was met with the assurance and support of God in the fellowship of the community.

To be sure, the world of the New England Puritans was complex and multifaceted.[22] For example, following from the covenant, the Puritan community demanded a strict obedience to both temporal and sacred laws. The pleasures of this life were to be rightly enjoyed, but enjoyed nevertheless. And contrary to a deriding conventional misconception, music, dancing, and the arts were necessary to life. There was a fullness to an earthly life, a fullness that was informed (as it only can be) by the relation of life to matters eternal.

RELIGION AND THE SPIRIT OF CAPITALISM

The verses from the sermon on the mount are fundamental to the Christian religious spirit. No matter what organizational or denominational form the religion may take, the guiding principle has been the renunciation of gaining riches in this world.

> Lay not up for yourselves treasures upon earth, where moth and rust doth corrupt, and where thieves break through and steal: but lay up for yourselves treasures in heaven, where neither moth nor rust doth corrupt, and where thieves do not break through nor steal: for where your treasure is, there will your heart be also. [Matthew 6:19–21]

In preparing for the eternal, the gaining of economic wealth is certainly a hindrance. In the history of Christianity, worldly affairs were of interest only to the extent that they prepared human beings for the kingdom of Heaven. And as the economic critic Kurt Samuelsson has noted, "Insofar as economic problems were considered, the aim was to subordinate business and enterprise to a rigorous Christian code of morality that obstructed and confined them."[23] When it came to economics, the resolve of the early Puritans was to lay up treasures in heaven and not on earth.

Yet, ever since Max Weber put forth his thesis on the relation of Protestantism to capitalism, scholars have tried to show that religion created the motivation for the development of capitalism. In his book *The Protestant Ethic and the Spirit of Capitalism*, Weber argued that the doctrine of the "calling" was the basis for psychological values and social norms that encouraged the acquisitive spirit.[24] He made the case for the view that Protestants—especially those committed to the Calvinist faith—were encouraged to think of their everyday work (in whatever occupation or business) as a means of glorifying God. Weber suggested that the intrinsic value of work and acquisitiveness was largely practiced wherever the Calvinist doctrine of predestination took effective hold. According to this thesis, then, religion exerted an important influence on the emergence and growth of capitalism in Europe and the United States.

The popularity of the Weber thesis is in large measure due to its rebuttal of the materialist interpretation of history. Weber was trying to answer Marx's assertion that such superstructural phenomena as religion are determined or conditioned by the economic mode of production. In contrast, Weber sought to show how religion, as embodied in Calvinistic Puritanism, affected the economy, as represented in the form and growth of capitalism. However, with the emerging awareness of the complexity of base and superstructure, and with the development of a Marxism that is also theological, the Weber thesis must be looked at anew. A theology of culture allows us to understand in a quite different way the relation of religion to the spirit of capitalism.

In a thorough critique of Weber's methodology, Samuelsson logically and empirically refutes that part of Weber's study which tries to show a causal connection between Protestantism and economic progress.[25] Samuelsson demonstrates in his own detailed historical analysis that it is impossible to make a causal correlation between those states that were predominantly Protestant and the engagement of their populations in capitalist expansion. Furthermore, he shows (contrary to Weber) that after the Reformation economic progress was not particularly marked in Protestant countries, especially in Calvinist countries. In concluding his analysis of this aspect of Weber's thesis, Samuelsson notes that no correlation between economic and religious trends in these countries can be established. Any economic expansion that took place in the eighteenth century (after the Reformation) derives from nonreligious factors. And, "in New England too, despite a correlation that certainly appears superficially strong, we have been unable to find anything suggesting the existence of a connection, in the deeper meaning of the word, between Puritanism and capitalism."[26]

Weber's research on the correlation between Puritanism and economic growth suffers from the defects of circular reasoning, faulty techniques of correlation, and the lack of precision in the concepts he employs. His definition of Protestantism shifts without placing it in historical context. His notion of capitalism, or "the spirit of capitalism," has different meanings in various parts of his discussion. However, it is Weber's ahistorical methodology of attempting to isolate a single factor in a prolonged and intricate pattern of development and correlating it with a vast aspect of the whole of history that destroys his own argument. Samuelsson writes:

> It is in general a hopeless undertaking to try to isolate one particular factor even from a relatively limited sequence of events, in one particular country and over a very short period of time, with the object of determining the extent to which the factor in question evolved in harmony with the general process under consideration, i.e., the degree of 'correlation' and 'covariation.' But Weber does not hesitate to embark on such an undertaking for so complex a phenomenon as Puritanism and for so wide a concept as economic development, not over a short period but over about four hundred years, not in a limited geographical region but over the Western world as a whole![27]

Outside of the effort to correlate religion and the development of capitalism, Weber's thesis rests on illustrating a religious motivation for an interest in this-worldly economic pursuits. His analysis is based, however, on a dubious treatment of the Christian concept of "calling." He asserted that the Calvinists made success in one's calling an outward and visible sign of spiritual grace. The basic problem with Weber's use of the Puritan doctrine of calling is that the concept has different meanings historically and even its meaning among Puritans, especially the early Puritans, is quite different from that ascribed to it by Weber. Thus, as H. M. Robertson notes, "Even if Weber is correct in his interpretation of the doctrine in its eighteenth-century manifestations, he is incorrect in projecting this back into the sixteenth century, when the doctrine wore an entirely different aspect."[28]

The concept of the calling is an expression of the traditional religious belief that we are called to our life on this earth by a divine providence. The Christian belief in the calling emphasized in particular that daily tasks are to be performed without striving for advancement and riches, and that our time is to be devoted to serving God and doing good. In fact, the pursuit of riches is thoroughly denounced. The Puritan conception of calling has no connection with the notion that the pursuit of business and success in worldly affairs is a mark of God's favor. The religious person, Richard Baxter declared, shall not choose the vocation in life that promises the maximum advantage in money or esteem, but that in which he or she can best serve God and most easily avoid sin.[29] We are to devote ourselves to those activities which best produce the greatest social benefit to others. To seek to influence God by means of work and worldly deeds is improper. The pilgrimage of the Puritan follows the words from the First Epistle of John (2:16–17): "For all that is in the world, the lust of the flesh, and the lust of the eyes, and the pride of life, is not of the Father, but is of the world. And the world passeth away, and the lust thereof: but he that doeth the will of God abideth for ever.''

The calling that Weber is describing certainly does not apply to all time, but is appropriate as a guide for the conduct of life in the later phases of the doctrine. In the course of capitalist development, the doctrine of the calling changed from an admonition against covetous ambition to a comfortable belief suitable for a commercial life. But among the early Puritans, the call was not an invitation to amass great riches; contrary to Weber's ahistorical treatment, it ''was an invitation to live the orderly and settled life ordained for one by God, and to perform all the duties pertaining to it.''[30] The calling for the early Puritans therefore discouraged covetousness and ambition.

> The ''calling'' did not embody a progressive ideal. The demand for an ordered life, for an innerworldly asceticism, which Puritanism made and expressed in the conception of the ''calling'' had no message of a capitalistic nature to give to the world. It placed in the forefront the age-long static ideal of content with the decrees of providence.[31]

The doctrine of the calling for the Puritans was a calling to life, for life itself to be lived in the presence of God. It was not a business calling, a calling to store up treasures on earth; such an activity, indeed, was condemned. Only later, in the time of Benjamin Franklin at the end of the eighteenth century, was the calling employed in the interest of business. ''Then a tragic thing happened. Capitalism saw the business significance of calling, removed the transcendental, other-worldly motive, and transformed the 'calling' into a job.''[32] Capitalism itself was responsible for a gradual modification and attrition of the Puritan doctrine.

In other words, religion in the United States (as embodied in the Puritan ethic) changed as a result of the increasing influence of capitalist economics. With the rise of a capitalist class bent on pecuniary accumulation, Puritanism became secularized. The capitalist spirit that developed did so in spite of the inhibitions of religion, or at least to the extent that Puritanism tempered its ethics on economic pursuits in the course of changing commercial demands in the United States. And with industrial capitalism (to say nothing about post-industrial, advanced capitalism), the Puritan ethic on economics all but disappeared. Capitalist economic activity has engendered religious changes, not the reverse as argued by Weber.

As capitalism developed, religion tended to adapt to the realities of the material world. However, this has always been the case.

> Just as St. Paul made Christianity more acceptable to the Hellenic world of his day by incorporating in it elements of Greek philosophy, and just as missionaries of the Catholic church in northern Europe smoothed the path for the conversion of the Vikings and other heathens by blurring as far as possible the

distinctions between the old gods and the new God, so did certain leaders of the Free Church movement, confronted with the task of winning over merchants and other business men, find themselves having to adopt as sympathetic a position as possible towards wealth and economic activity. They let it be understood and under the influence of the environment presumably believed themselves to be right—that in certain defined conditions the rich man had at least the same chance as the camel.[33]

Earlier, Augustine and Thomas Aquinas had seen that the world outside was otherwise constituted and that daily living demanded exceptions to the rules. Although Calvinism retained the basic anticapitalist theology of Christianity, Calvin's environment was, nevertheless, one of a business and money economy. The members of the rising bourgeoisie were also to be served by the church.

The new and rising bourgeoisie developed an appropriate economic ethic that extolled such virtues as industry and the accumulation of money. By the end of the eighteenth century in the United States, contrary to Weber's thesis, the commercial ethic of Benjamin Franklin was not a culmination of a Puritan ethic on work and wealth. A new business ethic was instead emerging in support of trade and commerce that was either antagonistic to Puritan theology or brought religious practice along with it in a process of secularization. Benjamin Franklin and the later captains of industry were drawing from and modifying a spirit of commerce, greed, and pecuniary success that existed long before Puritanism, outside of Christian religious ideals. This was a spirit of the Renaissance, a protest against the old order, a new creativeness and openness of inquiry, a sense of progress in all realms of politics and economics.[34] Freedom from external authority, including that of the church (Catholic and Protestant), was encouraged in the selection of practical and moral endeavors. Finally, in the United States, the hold of Puritan theology on everyday life was eroded. As Samuelsson observes, "In every department of life, the break with the old Puritan spirit was asserting itself: in the sciences (Franklin's explanation of the phenomenon of lightning and his invention of the lightning conductor were no mean contributions to the extinction of traditional religious conceptions), in art and music and literature, in personal and social intercourse, in habits and customs."[35] This was indeed a break with the past, with new religious faiths as well as the secularized philosophies of "enlightenment" playing their part in the creation of a moral order that was appropriate to developing capitalism.

The dominant ideology from Franklin's time on is that of religious secularity and economic materialism. The Enlightenment brought an emancipation from those themes (religious and otherwise) that were detrimental to capitalist development. The economic virtues that Franklin wished to infuse in others were secular virtues that had little place in Christian teachings. Business activity, particularly economic growth and expansion, became a virtue in itself. Property and riches now became the goals of the secularized individual in the secular society. Even the idea of providence was used to justify the pursuit of capitalist activity.[36] That capitalism and its secularized ethic could be guided by Divine Providence is the antithesis of Puritan theology and certainly marks its decay in modern history.

The obvious conclusion to be drawn in an evaluation of Weber's thesis, especially when applied to the later development of capitalism, is provided by Samuelsson, a conclusion in which we concur in light of the theology of cultural development:

> The economic views of the Puritans neither encouraged nor obstructed the spirit of capitalism. This spirit existed and throve quite independently of religious belief. Insofar as successful businessmen were also members of Puritan sects, they were not impelled to economic transactions by their religion. But sometimes they tried to construe these transactions, both to themselves and to others, in as favourable a religious light as possible; they thereby provided, to the confusion of posterity, an impression of a link that did not exist.[37]

Thus, the secularized pursuit of capitalist enterprise came to be justified, whenever a justification was needed, *ex post facto*, by religious or any other ideas that would seemingly support what capitalists desired to do in their worldly practice.

> The wholly secularized Carnegie, abjurer of Christian doctrine; the warmly religious Rockefeller; the nominally Protestant Jim Hall, whose largest donations went to Catholic institutions; John Jacob Astor and Cornelius Vanderbilt, to whom religious speculations were plainly unfamiliar; Ford the simple provincial: in all of them we find this singular and mongrel ideology. From a variety of philosophies they picked out whatever contributed to the defence of their own conduct, riches and power. Whether it was God or Franklin or some more generalized conception that was invoked, this ideological farrago stands revealed—insofar as it bears scrutiny at all—as a rationalization of accomplished facts rather than a motivating force.[38]

Ideas and beliefs gave support and defense to capitalism when the works of capitalists were already being accomplished. Strict compliance to the theology of early Puritanism would only have hindered the growth of capitalism.

This is far from concluding, on the other hand, that religion is solely a product of the substructure of capitalism. Like other elements of the "superstructure," especially that of art, an understanding of religion cannot be reduced to a materialist analysis of history. At most, religion is mediated by the material base of developing capitalism. As R. H. Tawney illustrated in his book, *Religion and the Rise of Capitalism*, there is a complex interaction between economic and religious changes.[39] To the degree that religion actually inhibits capitalist growth, it is definitely independent of the mode of production. Religion may, in fact, transcend the historical context of the material world. Indeed, it is the prophetic characteristic of religion that allows it to both transcend the material world (including the economic mode of production) and transform that world through its transcendence. As a way of being in the world in time and also apart from that temporality, religion is prophetic in its forms and content. The sacred makes a contribution to its own time in the transcending principle of the eternal.

However, the philosophies of the Enlightenment rather than Protestant theology played the central role in economic expansion and capitalist development. Rationalism, faith in capitalism, social Darwinism, economic liberalism—these were the systems of thought that cut across all religious creeds and gave impetus and ideological support to the development of capitalism.[40] The realities of mercantile trade and industrialization called forth an ideology that would condone the growing capitalist mode of production, often (and perversely) in the name of God. These realities of the material world gave rise to both the capitalist spirit and a secularized religious faith. Eventually the spirit of capitalism and secular religion became associated in the further development of capitalism.

Capitalism as a practice and as a theory replaced an agricultural and trade economy and an inner-worldly asceticism that gave sacred meaning to everyday life. The gradual transformation of Puritan ethics into capitalist motives worked to the detriment of the worker. The outcome is a mode of life that "has become rationalized upon a mechanical basis instead of upon a religious one."[41] The pursuit of capitalism has stripped our calling of its religious and moral meaning. That life has become associated with purely mundane passions was explicitly recognized and lamented by Weber in the conclusion of his work:

> Today the spirit of religious asceticism—whether finally, who knows?—has escaped from the cage. But victorious capitalism, since it rests on mechanical foundations, needs its support no longer. The rosy blush of its laughing heir, the Enlightenment, seems also to be irretrievably fading, and the idea of duty in one's calling prowls about in our lives like the ghost of dead religious beliefs. Where the fulfillment of the calling cannot directly be related to the highest spiritual and cultural values, or when, on the other hand, it need not be felt simply as economic compulsion, the individual generally abandons the attempt to justify it at all.[42]

This last stage of cultural development, Weber adds, is characterized by "specialists without spirit, sensualists without heart."

The diagnosis of what capitalism has wrought is essentially correct. What Weber failed to recognize is the redeeming power of grace through providence. What Weber ignored—or refused to admit (largely because of his own economic liberalism)—is the social and economic transformation that would be brought about in the development of socialism. The world is to be rebuilt in the socialist faith and struggle. A true religious spirit founded on and contributing to a socialist economy marks the new and emerging age. Divine Providence goes beyond capitalism to the expectant goal of socialism.

THE PURITAN THEOLOGY OF ROGER WILLIAMS

The American colonies were born of the revolution that was occurring in the material world. They were, in fact, a product of the more general European movement from feudalism to capitalism. The same material revolution in trade and economy that sent Columbus to America in 1492 culminated in the colonization of the native land by England. And the same material revolution that encouraged mercantile and territorial expansion was also a revolution in philosophy, a revolution that affected matters of the spirit. The Enlightenment notion that a natural causality governed the world, apart from a Divine guidance, was the ideology that went hand in hand with economic expansion. By the time the Puritans set sail for a new land, largely sponsored by European stock companies, the secularization of their world was already well underway. In their search, they were themselves a part of the movement that would eventually make their own religious doctrine obsolete.

The Puritan Roger Williams, himself in part a product of the movement, was at the same time a Puritan prophet who spoke of things to come. While the Puritan leaders of Massachusetts were conceding to the materialism of this world, Roger Williams was acting as a witness to a purity of life that only prophets can recognize. As archaic as his foundations may be today, in mind and in spirit, Roger Williams continues to be a source in our own reconstruction.

Upon being banished from the Massachusetts colonies, Williams and a small band of Puritans made their way southward in the winter of 1636, to the long exposure of the "winter miseries in a howling wilderness."[43] Williams had refused to keep silent about the problems encountered in establishing a sacred community in a secular world. While Williams was serving as the minister of a congregation in Salem, Governor Winthrop and the magistrates of Massachusetts became worried about the fact that Williams was attacking certain aspects of the emerging religious and political system. Williams, in being a more zealous and radical Puritan than the leading ministers of Massachusetts, openly preached against the Church of England and urged the members of the congregation to renounce any ties between their church and that of England. Moreover, Williams publicly avowed his belief that the magistrates had no authority to punish anyone for breaches of God's law as given in the Ten Commandments. He further preached that the settlers sinned in accepting a royal charter that used some impious language and purported to give title to land that actually belonged to the native inhabitants. From the standpoint of a radical Puritanism, Roger Williams was questioning the civil authority of the covenanted community.

The Puritan leaders were deeply disturbed by the preachings of Williams and feared that his ideas would disrupt the newly founded community. Although John Cotton, the most prominent minister in the colony, suggested that Williams's "violent course did spring rather from scruple of conscience than from sedious principle," Williams's attacks on the policies of the magistrates proved to be too much for the members of the General Court.[44] In the summer of 1635, Williams was summoned before the General Court, and during the course of the hearings his opinions were unanimously adjudged to be erroneous and dangerous. Upon Williams's refusal to recant, the governor pronounced the sentence of banishment.

The Puritan emphasis on the religious experience of personal and social life was only to be enhanced in the banishment. Making their way through the Plymouth colony into the wilderness region of Narragansett Bay, Williams and his companions finally reached the bank of the Seekonk River. Paddling in a canoe, the small party proceeded around the tip of a long ridge and rowed north to arrive at their destination. Landing at the sweet spring that flowed out of the west side of the ridge, Roger Williams called the place Providence. He would later write about the naming of Providence: "I desired it might be for shelter for persons distressed for conscience."[45] Providence was to be the blessing of God on the weary traveller and a refuge for the hunted and afflicted conscience. It was to represent the revelation of divine guidance, the hope and expectancy of religious experience. Roger Williams continued to draw from all of these purposes during his long, remaining years in this place.

Although the extent to which Roger Williams and his theology have affected history remains problematical, the attention he has received by interpreters of our past is considerable. The numerous and various treatments represent as much a history of the development of our own consciousness as a characterization of Roger Williams. For the last century he has been made out to be "an advocate of rational philosophy, the herald of modern humanism and individualism, a proponent of liberty in the Jeffersonian way—or even in the twentieth century way."[46] At other times, the portrait has been that of still another man: "To the Puritans and Puritan historians he was the troublemaker, 'the bad guy'; to other dissidents and their descendants—Baptists and Rhode Islanders—he was a martyr for freedom. To historians preoccupied with identifying democratic heros, he was the first great planter of democracy in America."[47] In recent years historians have come to appreciate the Puritanism of Roger Williams.

> By emphasizing Williams' essentially religious nature, historians of the 1950s and 1960s clearly demonstrated that Williams was a seventeenth-century man with seventeenth-century concerns. He was not an advocate of liberalism and democracy in the secular nineteenth– and twentieth-century understanding of those terms. His concern was not with this world, but the next. For him, as for all Puritans, what ultimately mattered was salvation. He differed from Massachusetts' Puritans only in his understanding of the means for achieving that salvation.[48]

A recognition of the radically religious Puritanism in the life and work of Roger Williams enables us to understand and appreciate the basic elements of his theology.

In order to understand the theology of Roger Williams we must recognize the central importance of the Bible in the life of the Puritan. As the theologian John Garrett has recently shown in his study of Williams, "The interaction of recurrent biblical themes enables us to share imaginatively in the way Roger Williams felt about his personal pilgrimage and the worlds of life and thought that were faced in his more than eighty stormy years."[49] In his searching of the Bible for the meaning of everyday affairs, Williams was profoundly different from the thinkers of the Enlightenment. Rather than looking to the laws of nature, Williams sought guidance in an understanding of God's plans as revealed in the Scriptures. And in distinction from Enlightenment beliefs, he acknowledged the need for government only as a temporary expedient until Jesus returned again to establish God's kingdom. As a Biblicist and Puritan, "his political thought must be considered within his intellectual frame of reference, which was primarily theological and religious."[50] Reformation of the world was to be in the light of God's word and under the guidance of the Holy Spirit.

Unlike the later framers of the Constitution, Roger Williams thought of all human beings as depraved and corrupt without hope of earthly remedy. He saw that supernatural enemy, the Devil, sitting masked in positions of authority—to be dethroned only when Christ returned. Thus,

> Williams was no optimistic "do it yourself Christian," with faith in America and the future. He looked on this life and everything in it as gross and worthless baubles and desired Eternity to be his business. He tackled practical commerce and politics without many illusions and regrets; but he wanted the Church to be virgin-pure.[51]

The political arena of this world was but a provisional space for us while we waited for religious life to be purified.

The Puritan expectation of Christ's second coming was both a conservative and a revolutionary idea. On the one hand, it gave approval to the legal compromises of duly constituted political authorities. As a religious person, Williams had no notion of creating a new kind of social order in this world. However, on the other hand, the coming of God's son who was killed on the Cross (by constituted authority) meant that there was to be an accounting; a judgment ultimately was to be made on how life was lived here on earth. There is a meaning in the universe. Only much later would the expectation of a socialist order, in light of this universal meaning, be integrated into the theological vision. But for Roger Williams, understandably, the existing order of the time would be the only one recognized.

Throughout his life Roger Williams was in constant search of religious purity. He was among those Calvinistic Seekers who call Christians to the duties of seeking and searching. By the time Williams found Providence, the words "search" and "seek" were already highly significant for him. His sympathies were with the oppressed exiles and the separated brethren who wandered in the wilderness seeking the millennial hope but not knowing how or when the millennium would arrive. John Garrett notes of Roger Williams, "It seemed to him that their posture was closer to Christ's sufferings and was more likely to be rewarded with His blessing, in the form of a Church renewed, when the time came for them to be delivered."[52] Williams soon doubted the validity of the church he himself founded in Providence in 1638. After a few months, he resigned from his church and again turned Seeker, to be alone without a church for the rest of his life. With the true Lord Jesus, he chose to stand with the hunted and the hurt, seeking God with his whole heart.

Roger Williams's vocation was that of itinerant preacher. As a witness to Christ and as a seeker willing to suffer the trials, Williams practiced his vocation (his life) all his years in colonial America. Piety was his whole life and was not segmented for special occasions. When John Winthrop asked him what he gained from his practices, he responded that he was trying to imitate Christ, witnessing to his future coming:

> I confess my gains, cast up in man's exchange, are loss of friends, esteem, maintenance, &c.: but what was gain in that respect I desire to count loss for the excellency of the knowledge of Christ Jesus my Lord, &c. To His all-glorious name I know that I have gained the honour of one of His poor witnesses, though in sackcloth.[53]

In the wilderness of the colonies, Williams sought the truly religious life of the missionary. As a modern day apostle he wandered among the people of this world, preparing the way for the new kingdom. This is how, Garrett writes, Roger Williams is to be assessed:

He thought of his own life as a vocation. He had been called by God to be a witness, and the form of obedience he followed must bring him close to the Cross. His model was Christ; therefore the coherent pattern of his career is best unravelled by reference to his understanding of the presentation of Christ's life and demands in the New Testament. Having chosen this standard, Williams declared he had found joyfulness and assurance.[54]

He sought the "powerless authority" that is revealed on the Cross, a rule that cannot be furthered by any political or religious establishment. Authority is in the Spirit. The prophet walks among us preparing the way for things to come.

In spite of his belief in religious tolerance ("soul liberty") and the free exchange of ideas, and of his belief in spiritual authority, Roger Williams was not an anarchist or laissez-faire liberal in the social and political affairs of this world. On the contrary, he thought that there was a need for strong political and social institutions to protect men and women from themselves in their secular activities. As one writer has observed, "Williams did not desire to alter civil and social relationships in secular things but sought to maintain them, believing that they were the instruments which preserved order in society."[55] Yet, Williams sought high standards of behavior for human affairs, suggesting that our relationships be characterized by love, mercy, self-sacrifice, and humility. Human society, nevertheless, was a human ordering rather than a sacral Christian institution.

Thus, fundamental to the political thought of Roger Williams is the distinction between the kingdom of Christ and the kingdoms of this world. Both are subject to and influenced by the sovereignty of God. But whereas the kingdom of Christ is the true Church, the politics of this world are watched over by God to the extent that people are given enough guidance to frame decent laws and set limits on excesses of authority. In other words, Williams gave no hint of the secular idealism of a later America. This aspect of Williams' theology is made clear in Garrett's observation:

> God had located the source of tolerably decent government in the people, as a defence against tyrants. By this divinely ordained means they would be protected from the consequences of their depravity and madness. Citizens should therefore respect and obey civil authorities, but not because of belief in the natural excellence of man and his institutions. The reason for a citizen's loyalty was acceptance of God's mercy in providing government as an alternative to the horrors his neighbours might devise if left to themselves.[56]

By disengaging the kingdom of Christ from the secular state, Williams was becoming a radical thinker about religion itself, but a conservative about the politics of this world. And, in the end, alas, "he looked so eagerly for a pure visible Church that the kind of Church he looked for became invisible to him."[57]

The problem with Williams's Puritan view of worldly politics is in its repudiation of the religious purposes of the state. Following Williams, government may in some ways reflect religious concerns, in subordination to God, but it requires skills and efforts that have little to do with religion.[58] In contrast to our ideas on the theology of culture, the separation of religion and the state leaves little room for considering the fulfillment of ultimate concerns through social institutions. The relative importance of Williams's theology is that, given the nature of some states, particularly the capitalist state of today, it is well not to conceive of the state as a holy instrument of God. State policies cannot be sanctified by religion, which would be a gross misuse of religion. Yet, what is diminished in Williams political thought (in relation to his theology) is the positive intellectual and religious framework for moving beyond an existing and oppressive social order. That framework is developing only now in the construction of a socialist theology.

But the expectant hope of the prophet has prevailed. Roger Williams did not escape into disembodied piety. As Garrett notes in his study of Williams, there was no postponement of action until kingdom come. The state of Rhode Island that formed around the founding of Providence still bears the mark of Roger Williams's Puritan theology, with faith and hope, and the anchor in heaven:

> The anchor which still appears on the crest of the state of Rhode Island appears to have its Puritan ancestry in a text in *Hebrews* (6.19–20) which calls this hope "an anchor of the soul." The strange location of this "anchor" in heaven turned the imagination of the Puritans upside down. While on earth they seemed to labour on a stormy sea, but they believed they were on the end of a line that held them fast and would finally guarantee them anchorage in a haven beyond all storms. The very narrowness of their heavenly religion gave them scope for action on a broad earthly horizon.[59]

The Puritans knew that everything they did had meaning for eternity. The anchor is in heaven.

In spite of substantive aspects of Roger Williams's theology that are objectionable to our current theological and socialist consciousness, there remains a prophetic theology in Puritanism that is vital to the present day reconstruction of social and moral life. Not that Puritanism will likely return; it is based on an archaic and outdated political economy. But the religious concern of the radical, revolutionary Puritan sects can be recovered and renewed. Prophetic theology provides us with the hopeful expectancy of things to come, revealed in light of the eternal. History, we know, is the divine presence through the people of this world. The social and moral order we create is a revelation of the sacred.

NOTES

1. James Luther Adams, *On Being Human Religiously: Selected Essays in Religion and Society*, ed. and intro. Max L. Stackhouse (Boston: Beacon Press, 1976), p. 248.
2. Paul Tillich, *The Protestant Era* (Chicago: University of Chicago Press, 1948), p. xvii.
3. Adams, *On Being Human Religiously*, p. 245.
4. Raymond Williams, "Base and Superstructure in Marxist Cultural Theory," *New Left Review*, no. 82 (November–December, 1973), p. 5.
5. On cultural creations as practices, see Ibid., pp. 13–16.
6. See James West Davidson, *The Logic of Millennial Thought: Eighteenth-Century New England* (New Haven: Yale University Press, 1977), pp. 3–12.
7. Ibid., p. 17, quoting Jonathan Edwards.
8. Alan Heimert, *Religion and the American Mind: From the Great Awakening to the Revolution* (Cambridge: Harvard University Press, 1966), pp. 64–66.
9. Ernest Lee Tuveson, *Millennium and Utopia: A Study in the Background of the Idea of Progress* (Berkeley: University of California Press, 1949), p. 112.
10. J. H. Hexter, *The Judaeo-Christian Tradition* (New York: Harper & Row, 1966), pp. 98–99.
11. Christopher Hill, *The World Turned Upside Down: Radical Ideas During the English Revolution* (New York: Viking Press, 1972), p. 74.
12. Hexter, *The Judaeo-Christian Tradition*, p. 96.
13. Hill, *The World Turned Upside Down*, p. 76.
14. Ibid., p. 75, quoting Arise Evans.
15. Ibid., p. 123.
16. Ibid.
17. Ibid., pp. 296–300.
18. Winthrop S. Hudson, "Puritanism and the Spirit of Capitalism," *Church History*, 18 (March, 1949), p. 9, quoting Richard Baxter.
19. Ibid., p. 10, quoting Baxter.
20. Ibid., p. 14.
21. Page Smith, *As a City upon a Hill: The Town in American History* (New York: Alfred A. Knopf, 1966), pp. 3–14.
22. See the following description of the New England Puritan community: "Given such widespread disagreement, then, I should make clear—albeit perhaps a bit belatedly—what I have meant and will mean when writing of the New England Puritan community. I am writing of those seventeenth- and eighteenth-century New Englanders who generally shared the religious beliefs of their congregational ministers—from John Cotton to Cotton Mather to Jonathan Edwards; who believed in human depravity, predestination, and God's inscrutability; who believed in the divine inspiration for their mission in the new New World; and who labored at their earthly tasks with these beliefs ever before them, finding in their experiences portents of God's pleasure or displeasure and indications of his millennial plan. *Further, and perhaps most important, they held these beliefs in tandem with a growing sense of unease with, and isolation from, the developing worldliness, liberalism, and secularism of the larger*

society in which they were living" (Emphasis added). From David E. Stannard, *The Puritan Way of Death: A Study in Religion, Culture, and Social Change* (New York: Oxford University Press, 1977), p. 136.

23. Kurt Samuelsson, *Religion and Economic Action: A Critique of Max Weber*, trans. E. Geoffrey French (New York: Harper & Row, 1964), p. 151.
24. Max Weber, *The Protestant Ethic and the Spirit of Capitalism*, trans. Talcott Parsons (New York: Charles Scribner's Sons, 1958).
25. Samuelsson, *Religion and Economic Action*, pp. 96–147.
26. Ibid., p. 120.
27. Ibid., p. 150.
28. H. M. Robertson, "A Criticism of Max Weber and His School," in Robert W. Green (ed.), *Protestantism and Capitalism: The Weber Thesis and Its Critics* (Boston: D.C. Health, 1959), p. 69.
29. See Samuelsson, *Religion and Economic Action*, p. 37.
30. Robertson, "A Criticism of Max Weber and His School," p. 70.
31. Ibid., p. 71.
32. Kemper Fullerton, "Calvinism and Capitalism" *Harvard Theological Review*, 21 (July, 1928), p. 191.
33. Samuelsson, *Religion and Economic Action,,* p. 29.
34. See Ibid., pp. 48–50. Also see R. H. Tawney, *Religion and the Rise of Capitalism* (New York: Harcourt Brace Jovanovich, 1926).
35. Ibid., p. 53.
36. See Jacob Viner, *The Role of Providence in the Social Order: An Essay in Intellectual History* (Princeton, N.J.: Princeton University Press, 1972).
37. Samuelsson, *Religion and Economic Action*, p. 42.
38. Ibid., p. 78.
39. Tawney, *Religion and the Rise of Capitalism*.
40. Samuelsson, *Religion and Economic Action*, pp. 151–152.
41. Fullerton, "Calvinism and Capitalism," pp. 193–194.
42. Weber, *The Protestant Ethic and the Spirit of Capitalism*, pp. 181–182.
43. For various accounts, see Sydney V. James, *Colonial Rhode Island: A History* (New York: Charles Scribner's Sons, 1975), pp. 13–32; Edwin C. Rozwenc, *The Making of American Society*, vol. 1 (Boston: Allyn and Bacon, 1972), pp. 68–75; Sydney E. Ahlstron, *A Religious History of the American People* (New Haven: Yale University Press, 1972), pp. 166–183.
44. Rezwenc, *The Making of American Society*, p. 70.
45. Ahlstrom, p. 167, quoting Roger Williams. The writings of Roger Williams are contained in the seven volumes of *The Complete Works of Roger Williams* (New York: Russell and Russell, 1966).
46. Mauro Calamandrei, "Neglected Aspects of Roger Williams' Thought," *Church History*, 21 (September, 1952), p. 240.
47. Nancy E. Peace, "Roger Williams—A Historiographical Essay," *Rhode Island History*, 35 (November, 1976), p. 109.
48. Ibid., p. 110.
49. John Garrett, *Roger Williams: Witness Beyond Christendom, 1603–1683* (New York: Macmillan, 1970), p. 2.
50. Peace, "Roger Williams—A Historical Essay," p. 107.
51. Garrett, *Roger Williams*, p. 8.
52. Ibid., p. 51.
53. Ibid., p. 46, quoting Roger Williams.
54. Ibid., p. 240.

55. Robert D. Brunkow, "Love and Order in Roger Williams' Writings," *Rhode Island History*, 35 (November, 1976), p. 115.
56. Garrett, *Roger Williams*, p. 243.
57. Ibid.
58. See Edmund S. Morgan, *Roger Williams: The Church and the State* (New York: Harcourt, Brace & World, 1967), pp. 115–120.
59. Garrett, *Roger Williams*, p. 247.

3
Capitalist Development and the Secularization of Religion

The essence of all true religion lies in holy love; and in this divine affection and an habitual disposition to it and that light which is the foundation of it and those things which are the fruits of it, consists the whole of religion.
JONATHAN EDWARDS, *A Treatise Concerning Religious Affections*, 1746

The Puritan myth continues to hold our imagination even in the most secular of times. We are now beyond any source that could portray the actuality of Puritan life and religion. What we have, instead, is a referent in our history that allows us to construct anew a sensibility that has the hope of leading us out of the current malaise of capitalist existence. The essence of Puritan theology and the prophetic mode is to be found in our own need and imagination.

The continuing relevance of Puritanism and its immense historical importance was described by Perry Miller when he wrote that "it was not only the most coherent and most powerful single factor in the early history of America, it was a vital expression of a crucial period in European development, and those who would understand the modern world must know something of what it was and of what heritages it has bequeathed to the present."[1] The thought and spirit of seventeenth and early eighteenth century New England reflect the most important problems of the epoch. The struggles of that time and place have not only left their mark on our present but provide a basis for moving beyond the spiritual and material problems of our own age.

The Puritan struggle was one of reconciling faith with reason and of adapting that reconciliation to material and productive existence. Immigration to New England was an experiment in the founding of a social and moral order that would place material need in the context of a pious life. Although the early Puritans were still dominated by spiritual considerations, their piety was nevertheless tempered by the experiment of living in New England. Puritanism, moreover, had developed out of a much larger intellectual and spiritual environment. Even at its highest intensity, "Puritanism had never cast off a rich and complicated intellectual heritage, though it had tried to simplify certain departments; Puritans still believed not only in their religious creed, but in reason, logic, and the arts."[2] By the time the colonies were founded, and in the course of their founding, the emotional drive of Puritan piety was on the wane. From then on, the Puritans made a deliberate effort to combine their piety with their intellectual concepts and to harmonize this dialectic with the existential necessity of living in the material world. The problem persists for us today.

The balance of material (especially economic) life with the spiritual was the task of the second and all subsequent generations of Puritans. With these generations, New England becomes more than a colony of Europe; it becomes local and a province. The daily difficulties of hard work, administration of church and community despite interference from England—all these challenges had to be confronted in a new setting. Amid "your eating & marriage . . . your buying & selling, your plowing and howing, your sowing & mowing and reaping, your feeding cattle and keeping sheep, your planting orchards & gardens, your baking and brewing, your building houses or outhouses, your fencing in ground or other business what ever," amid all these are to be found the conditions of religious experience.[3]

Although the agricultural and mercantile economy of the colonies was developing gradually into a primitive, nascent capitalism (before eventually evolving to industrial capitalism), Puritanism made no easy alliance with materialism and the acquisitive spirit. Although there might be statements from some pulpits that could be interpreted as favorable to commercial and business interests, the Puritan ethic was uncongenial to anything that might be called "the spirit of capitalism."[4] But adjustments had to be made. A world system economy of trade, commerce, and private entrepreneurship left little room for anything other than the development of a local capitalist economy. And given the complete absence of the material basis for any form resembling socialism, as well as the absence of a socialist consciousness, adjustments had to be made to the only material existence available—that of developing capitalism.

Material existence involved an alliance with the political as well as the economic world. In this realm, the Puritan notion of the convenant of grace emerged as a philosophy of a national covenant.[5] Federal theologians worked out a philosophy that had God entering into a covenant not only with individuals in a social group, but with the public and the emerging political state. Members of the community, accordingly, entered into a legal contract with God through the material apparatus of the state. The federal idea was being inserted into the substance of divinity; the basis of the relation of God to the individual and to the group was being changed from spiritual necessity to legal contract. The rationalism of the Enlightenment merged concretely with the development of the capitalist state. The spirit of Puritanism adjusted to the national trend and at the same time gave support to it in the course of its own secularization.

This, then, is the course of New England and the rest of the country: a secularization of life with emphasis on matters economic and political. An environment infused with the religious decreased with the further secular development of the United States. The religious experience of daily life gave way to a secular existence with religion relegated to segmented portions of life. There is thus a general and pervasive displacement of religious interpretations of reality by an orientation that seeks explanations of social and moral life in rational and scientific terms.[6] Search for meaning is no longer confined within the spiritual realm or within religious institutions. Emphasis is placed instead on an objective faith in rationality and a trust in that which is empirically observable. The earth and the human beings on it become the center of a finite universe. Existence in a capitalist society becomes the measure of all things.

Yet the subterranean strain of religious experience continued to show itself at crucial points in the development of the United States. The rationalism espoused by the liberal bourgeoisie has been constantly challenged by the religious response. Evangelical religion, most notably expressed for us by Jonathan Edwards in the Great Awakening of the 1740s, provides a radical affirmation of the essence of life. The dialectic between faith and reason continues to be recharged by the recurrence of the sacred, by the recognition that the source of life, finite and eternal, is found ultimately in the transcendent spirit. Given the appropriate conditions, a socialist existence will come as much by spirit as by reason—by both in their wholeness.

THE RISE OF ENLIGHTENMENT

The American colonies were born not only out of emerging capitalism, but out of the Enlightenment as well. The voyage to the New World, made possible by the social and economic growth of capitalism, was given impetus by intellectual and scientific advances. The Enlightenment emphasized a mastery of the material world in order to serve humanity (especially certain portions of it). In rejecting the dogma of the medieval world, in challenging the existing order, the ideas of the Enlightenment helped to open frontiers in many realms, from those of territorial geography, to frontiers of mind and spirit. "To reach the truth one must," asserted Descartes, "once in one's life, dispense with all received opinions, and reconstruct anew and from the foundations all one's systems of knowledge."[7]

The ideas of the Enlightenment spread rapidly in the American colonies. As Herbert Aptheker has observed in his study of the period, "Here was a land whose birth was a product of the movement from feudalism to capitalism; hence it was to be expected that the philosophical offspring of that revolution would find welcome here."[8] Enlightenment thought coupled with capitalist development found its purest expression in the early period of colonization and the movement to the founding of the nation. Freedom of expression and freedom of economic experimentation and growth were the necessary ingredients for early capitalist development. "The Enlightenment—epitomized in the realization that all is subject to change and that nature's laws can be mastered by man for his greater happiness—combined with a rudimentary sense of nationalism, forging the revolutionary patriot."[9]

In other words, the development of capitalism was a part of the passage from a "supernaturalistic-mythical-authoritative to the naturalistic-scientific-individualistic type of thinking."[10] During the eighteenth century, in the emerging nation of the United States as well as in the established European countries, the Western world turned from the Middle Ages to "modern" times. And in this new modern world, the nature of God changed also. The place of the sacred in daily life was altered, diminishing the extent to which religion pervaded an understanding of essential order in the universe.

Proof of order in the universe now depended more on the faculties of reason rather than those of faith. Human progress, accordingly, was a product of the reasoning mind. Faith tended to be distrusted and relegated to the realm of the irrational. Advances in knowledge and science were to be founded on a materialist outlook and an empirical method of observation. Enlightenment ideas were thus fused into a new "religion of humanity."

The now famous couplet by Alexander Pope, dating from the early 1730s, sets the tone for the new emphasis on secular humanity: "Know then thyself, presume not God to scan: The Proper study of Mankind is Man."[11] Philosophers from Hume to Kant to Locke gave prominence to the "study of man." Theological interpretations of life—once the intellectual as well as spiritual basis of Christian culture—tended to give way to the science of human behavior. "The science of human nature," Pope wrote, "is like all other sciences, reduced to a few clear points."[12] This was a scientific humanism that not only reduced human life to laws of the natural and physical world, but placed the human being at the center of a secular, finite universe.

In freeing human life (in theory and practice) from the external authority of religion, license was given to individualistic enterprise. Secular life was no longer subordinate to religious codes of conduct. The result was the freedom to engage in unrestricted commercial pursuits; separate now from a religious morality were rationalism, faith in capitalism, and laissez-faire enterprise. The necessary intellectual, spiritual, and cultural foundation was being laid for the further development of capitalism.

The body of Enlightenment thought that became known as liberalism was entirely appropriate for the rising bourgeoisie of Europe and

America. Because the human world was visualized as "an agglomeration of autonomous individuals each seeking his own self-interest by increasing his pleasures and decreasing his pains," society was conveniently considered a body of competitors who entered into contractual arrangements with one another to satisfy individual and sometimes mutual interests.[13] The social and moral order represented the sum of individual needs and material goods. Happiness gained through private property and its pursuit was the most basic natural right. And capitalism—with the means of production in private hands—was the natural and best means of social and moral progress. The liberalism of the Enlightenment was thus made to correspond with, and to serve the interests of, the emerging capitalist class. Liberalism promoted capitalism and a capitalist class; and capitalism in turn secured and perpetuated the liberal, secular philosophy of human life and society. Liberalism was (and continues to be) the moral source and product of developing capitalism, a secular philosophy for a capitalist class.

The stance of the Enlightenment—as it continued into the nineteenth century—toward religion was that religion may never disappear, but it certainly must be transformed. After the experience of the French Revolution, religion was attacked on the grounds that it should be transformed into a tool of social utility. The liberal philosophes sought to devise a religion "which would be, at one and the same time, scientifically credible, psychologically satisfying, and socially useful."[14] The "religion of humanity" spread from the positivistic treatments of Saint-Simon and Auguste Comte to such very different groups as the philosophical radicals and the Young Hegelians. In all versions, the religion of humanity rested on faith in "man" and on stable political structures of the emerging capitalist nation-states. Religion was, in fact, to be used to promote these secular faiths and institutions. Collective humanity, organized into the capitalist political economies, became the principal reality of the nineteenth and twentieth centuries. The individual human being had become God. There were few traces left of a transcendent Being.

The sense that we have now, however, in the last decades of the twentieth century, is that we are living at the end of an era. Over a century ago the German theologican Friedrich Schleiermacher, in response to the ethos embodied in the new religion of humanity, pointed the direction, saying that "the Reformation must continue." Taking up the reformation theme again in this century, Paul Tillich (recognizing the end of the secular era of the Enlightenment) forged a theology rooted in "the Reformation assertion of the unconditional character of God and in the idea that the fulfillment of human existence ultimately depends not upon human device and mediations (of Catholic, Protestant, or secular type) but rather upon justification through faith."[15] Tillich sought to give the faith doctrine a restatement in modern terms.

The objective is to go beyond the rational-secular control of nature and society, an Enlightenment idea that supported capitalism. The spirit of "self-sufficient finitude" is to be replaced with a renewed relationship to the infinite, by a reconciliation of existence and essence. The Judeo-Christian prophetic belief in providence is to be restored and transformed. If religion is to play a prophetic and creative role in moving beyond the decaying Enlightenment era, there must be a break with the capitalist ethos—replacing it with a religious-socialist principle.

Our problem today is to find an unconditional ground for all that exists conditionally. The world wrought by advanced, secular capitalism and supported by dying Enlightenment ideas is faced with problems that are essentially religious. We are at the end of an era. The task of a prophetic theology—and a religious life—is to create the epoch that must certainly replace the one that is passing.

FROM COLONIAL TO INDUSTRIAL CAPITALISM

Early capitalism was stimulated and given the necessary intellectual and spiritual support by the secular Enlightenment. Trade, commerce, and exploration among the European nations in the sixteenth and seventeenth centuries provided the material bases for procedures and forms that were unimaginable before that time, including commodity production and capital accumulation. The economic formation that we now know as the capitalist mode of production was made possible by the breakdown of feudal economic forms, the expansion of national empires, and the simultaneous growth of new ideas of a secular nature.

A series of transformations took place in the transition from feudalism to capitalism which resulted in a new social division of labor. Most important were the separation of the commercial (and eventually the industrial) from the agricultural, a distinction between manual and mental labor, and an opposition between the city and the country.[16] Mercantilism—by protecting enrerprise within the nation—further enhanced the early development of capitalism. The colonies of the mercantile nations served as markets for exports and suppliers of raw materials to the mother countries. The extension of commerce into a world market system opened a new phase in the historical development of capitalism.

True to their mercantile interests, the merchants and manufacturers of England were able to secure a series of acts controlling the economic activity of the American colonies.[17] The parliamentary legislation restrained the manufacture of some colonial goods, such as woolens and iron, which would have competed with English manufacturing, and encouraged other colonial goods, such as naval stores (tar, pitch, turpentine, resin, and hemp) which were needed as raw materials in English manufacturing. As the economy of England developed, the list of controlled commodities shifted to satisfy English commerical interests. But such control was by no means complete nor in the end effective. For despite the imperial aims of England, and as a result of the vigorous enterprise on the part of colonial merchants, the American economy grew rapidly. By the mid–1700s a colonial economy was, in fact, competing successfully with England. The flourishing economy of colonial capitalism was fast becoming a source of strain and conflict with the mercantile system of the British empire. The American colonies were establishing their own capitalist economy.

Capitalist development of the American colonies inevitably meant political and economic independence from England. This was the contradiction built into the mercantile-colonial relationship between England and her colonies in North America. The American Revolution was the consequence of the contradiction in the mercantile-colonial economic relationship.[18] Further capitalist development of the colonies required severing the relationship and forming an autonomous bourgeois political state. With the establishment of the United States, the nation (although still predominantly mercantile, protecting itself from its foreign competition) was on its way to becoming a developed capitalist society. All the characteristics we now associate with capitalism—including class structure and labor exploitation—were set in motion.

Capitalism, as a system of production based on the exploitation of a working class by the capitalist class that owns and controls the means of production, is a dynamic system that has gone through various stages of development in the subsequent history of the United States. Capitalism has constantly transformed its own forces and relations of production; the whole of capitalist society is constantly being altered within the basic framework of capitalist political economy. Thus, capitalism is always affecting the social existence of all who live under it.[19] This is the basic dynamic of capitalist development, an interdependence between production, the relations of production, and the social structure of institutions.

An understanding of the social and moral order of capitalism necessarily involves an investigation of the relationship between the development of capitalism and the social relations that correspond to this development. Moreover, as capitalism has developed, there has been an increasing discrepancy between the productive forces and the capitalist relations of production. Economic expansion, fundamental to capitalism, exacerbates rather than mitigates the contradictions of capitalism.[20] Workers are further exploited and conditions of existence worsen, while the contradictions of capitalism increase. Capitalist development, in other words, and from another vantage point, creates the conditions for the transformation and abolition of capitalism, brought about in actuality by class struggle.

The United States has developed gradually as a capitalist society. The nascent capitalist economy of the colonial stage of American capitalism was, by and large, an economy of farming, shipping, and commerce. As manufacturing became increasingly important, the population grew rapidly and the urban centers grew in size and importance. Immigration continued to increase to supply the needed labor for manufacturing in the growing factory system. From the time of the American Revolution to the Civil War, the United States was becoming a major industrial nation. The remainder of the nineteenth century was marked by unprecedented economic growth and expansion, making the United States the leading nation of industrial capitalism.[21]

Nevertheless, or as a consequence of the contradictions of capitalist development, the nation was beset with recurring economic depressions and recessions, most notably in the years 1819, 1837, 1839, 1857, 1873, and 1893. More and more people were being adversely affected by developing capitalism. And by the turn of the century it was becoming clear that industrial capitalism must be regulated and supported by the developing capitalist state. Advanced capitalism was reaching a point of increasing crisis—economic, social, and moral—brought about by the contradictions inherent in the capitalist system of production and control.

The social and moral life in capitalist society—today as in the past—is affected not only by the economic conditions of production, but also by the struggle between classes produced by these conditions. For the capitalist system to operate and survive, the capitalist class must exploit the labor of the working class. The capitalist class survives by appropriating this labor, and the working class exists as long as labor power is required in the productive process. Moreover, the amount of labor appropriated, the techniques of labor exploitation, the conditions of working-class life, and the level of working-class consciousness have all been an integral part of the historical development of capitalism. Class conflict thus permeates the whole of capitalist development. The history of the development of capitalism in the United States is the history of class struggle.

Throughout the colonial era a class-divided society was gradually being created. Already the contradictions of early capitalism were being manifested in the antagonisms between slaves and indentured servants, farmers, artisans, laborers, and mechanics—on the one hand—and merchants, plantation owners, and a rising petite bourgeoisie on the other.[22] A plantation economy in the Southern colonies required a mass importation of labor, black slaves from Africa. By 1775 about a half million slaves were being used in the colonies. As manufacturing increased a growing population of laborers—yeoman farmers in the colonies and workers imported from European countries—were crowding into the cities to supply labor for factories. The further development of capitalism in the United States only served to widen the gap and increase the class conflict between the vast working population and the rising capitalist class that owned and controlled the means of production.

A few merchant families in the colonies, such as the Browns of Providence, Rhode Island, set the pace for the early development of a capitalist class. With great display of inventiveness and entrepreneurship, these early capitalists charted the course from merchant shipping (including the slave trade) to industrialization. The Browns went into business in 1723 as merchants in the maritime trade; by the time of the Revolution they had become well-established manufacturers. With the element of rationality, embodied in the enlightened spirit of capitalism, the Browns planned their economic future: "Motivated by the desire to build a business which could be passed on to future generations of the family, they were bound whenever possible to take the long view. They sought stability rather than short-term profits, and their day-to-day plans were geared to this general objective."[23]

The social and moral order that emerged from the development of capitalism in the period 1790 to 1860, the period of early industrialization, was shaped by the conditions of capitalist exploitation. A society increasingly devoid of religious concern, a society increasing secular, gave primacy to the capitalistic values of acquisitiveness, competition, and the ability to justify exploitation. The conditions of the working population continued to deteriorate in the course of industrialization. As Jurgen Kuczynski has shown in his study of the historical statistics, the working day for laborers was being lengthened during this period, women and children were being drawn into the factories, and the actual working conditions were growing worse.[24] In the course of the capitalist exploitation during this early period of industrialization, however, workers were beginning to alter their traditional conceptions of work and were forming a consciousness appropriate for a working class in an industrializing, capitalist society. Not only was a working class being created in the course of capitalist development, but a class consciousness of workers sharing a common condition was also forming.[25]

The United States was fast becoming the greatest industrial power of the world. During the years 1860 to 1900, continually at the expense of the working class, production grew, and the accumulation of capital among the capitalist class mounted. However, the conditions of the newly freed black workers were not improved; they were faced with insufficient wages, poor housing conditions, low standards of health, and crowding in cities. Immigrant laborers and their families were exploited at the work place as well as at home. Although there was some improvement in real wages during this period of capitalist development, health conditions grew worse, housing deteriorated, the accident rate in industry increased, and the gap between the capitalist class and the working class widened.[26] At the same time, and largely because of growing capitalist exploitation, workers increased their struggle against capitalist conditions. The workers' chief weapon was the strike, and it was used frequently during the last years of the nineteenth century. In 1886, as the eight-hour movement was taking place, there were 1,572 strikes and lock-outs involving 610,024 employees against 11,562 establishments. With other actions as well, such as the slow-down and the boycott, workers were struggling against the particular social and moral order that was being created in the development of capitalism.

As capitalism developed beyond the industrial stage, becoming dominated by large corporations after 1900, the conditions of labor were even more adversely affected. Increasing technology only served to further alienate workers from the work process. Especially after World War I, with the coming of the economic depression, unemployment among workers increased. Rising unemployment continued to plague advanced capitalism as the general economy moved from one crisis to another. Even before World War II, the life of the American worker showed the consequences of a decaying capitalist system: "The worker's life tends more and more to be composed of a short period of years, during which he produces with unprecedented intensity, and of a long period during which he works at a considerably reduced rate of speed, often interrupted by illness, and at a much lower wage."[27] The struggle between the capitalist and the working class grew in intensity during the postwar period. Yearly strikes now included millions of workers, involving the range of workers—from industrial employees to white-collar and public service employees. Class struggle and class consciousness continue to intensify as capitalism reaches the final stages of development.

Advanced capitalism has achieved a character of its own in relation to the basic class struggle. In the late stage of capitalist development the state has expanded and increased its role in securing the capitalist system. The state is necessary at this advanced stage to ensure the continuation of capital accumulation.[28] The state must also cope with the surplus population that results from the contradictions of advanced capitalism. Ultimately, however, the capitalist state cannot sustain private capital accumulation and, at the same time, legitimize the relations of advanced capitalism. The modern capitalist state, as well as the capitalist economic system, is in a crisis that will continue to increase as long as the capitalist system resists transformation into a socialist society.

The dialectic of the class struggle assures a conflict within advancing capitalist society. In not only failing to eliminate class struggle but, in fact, increasing it, the capitalist state contains the contradictions for its own demise. While the function of state control is expanding, larger portions of the population are becoming politicized. Especially for the "unproductive" segments of the population (those whose labor does not result directly in profits for capitalists), there is increased involvement in the class struggle. For state workers, the unemployed, and welfare recipients—all growing portions of the population—a political consciousness develops around their condition, a consciousness that questions the legitimacy of the existing system. The entire working class, productive and unproductive, is now joined in a common political struggle.

The role that religion will play in this struggle, however, is yet to be realized. Because the development of capitalism has also meant the secularization of religion, even the relegation of religion to a minor place in human social and moral life, we are left with few religious resources in our immediate past from which to draw. This makes the restoration of religious concern to the socialist movement even more acute—for socialism also (along with developing capitalism) has failed to attend to necessary religious needs. The socialist struggle requires a religious consciousness as much as a class consciousness. The transition to socialism is both political and religious. And ultimately the religious goal is one that transcends concrete political structures. The prophetic expectation speaks finally to that which is infinite and eternal.

A NATION UNDER GOD

As capitalism developed in the United States, religion became secularized along political as well as economic lines. The Puritan notion of the covenanted community—of settlers in a special compact with God and each other—was expanded to include the nation itself as a covenanted community. The gathering together of primary covenanted communities into a larger "secondary community" (the nation), was finally incorporated into the Constitution of the United States. The framers of the Constitution "were engaged in drafting a *secular* covenant, and the indispensable prelude to this covenant was a common spirit, a unity of interest and affection greater than any apparent divisions."[29] The federal constitution, in a secularization of the Puritan covenant, was invested with sacred qualities. An attack against the nation became also an assault against the national covenant, incorporating religious overtones. The political realm, represented by the motto "a nation under God," was a secularization of Puritanism, just as the "calling" to life was secularized in the economic realm as capitalism developed in the United States.

That Puritanism should become secularized politically was quite natural, given the colonists' hope that some day the new world would become fully Christian. An objective of the colonists, after all, was that religion and civilization would be wed—establishing a kingdom on earth in preparation for the final revelation.[30] The American Revolution came—in concept and rhetoric—as a progression toward establishing a Christian America. The belief that the nation needed a unifying religious perspective and a broadly accepted morality (however secular) continued in the subsequent intertwining of religious and national development in the United States.

For the original Puritan mind, "it was not possible to segregate a man's spiritual life from his communal life."[31] The Puritans founded the colonies for religious reasons, combining civil and ecclesiastical matters from the beginning. Their philosophy of the state was simply that human beings must establish a government which, in turn, would have the full power to enforce obedience. While each person had to work out his or her own salvation, the Puritan philosophy demanded that in society people need to be united into one political unit. As Perry Miller observes: "The theorists of New England thought of society as a unit, bound together by inviolable ties; they thought of it not as an aggregation of individuals but as an organism, functioning for a definite purpose, with all parts subordinate to the whole, all members contributing a definite share, every person occupying a particular status."[32] And regarding the state: "The state to them was an active instrument of leadership, discipline, and, wherever necessary, of coercion; it legislated over any or all aspects of human behavior, it not merely regulated misconduct but undertook to inspire and direct all conduct."[33] In the development of the United States, this political philosophy was elevated to the level of the nation-state. What once was a theory for the small, covenanted community became the political theory for the whole nation. The Puritan idea of the political community was being taken far beyond its original purpose. Any connection between society and religion was becoming unwieldy.

It is one thing to believe that God engenders the community by acting through the people, and that the people will abide by erected regulations with willing consent and active participation. It is quite another, however, to assume that the same process can take place on the national level, beyond the primary community. Yet this is what happened as the United States developed. The religious basis for the operation of the community was used to justify and sanction obedience to the emerging capitalist state. Citizens were led to believe that their subjection to national authority was divinely inspired. Religion—indeed, a truly secularized use of religion—was giving support and legitimacy to the nation and to its developing capitalist economy. In the Puritan sense, the relationship between community and religion had become severed.

As the colonies moved toward the Revolution, Puritan theology was adapted to the requirements of nationhood. A recognizable type of "enlightened" Christianity emerged. Its chief characteristics included an emphasis on the human role in redemption (Arminianism), a philosophical analysis of morality, a deprecation of evangelical ministry, an optimism about human progress, an impersonal relation to God, and a paramount faith in human reason.[34] The basic intellectual and religious trend of the eighteenth century, although there were marked dissident movements (especially in the Great Awakening of the 1740s), was that of enlightenment. Rationalism was extended into religion, modifying Puritanism, and the rational principle was integrated into the move for an independent nation. The "founding fathers" were men of the new rationalism who drew upon an enlightened and secularized theology to prepare the way for a common and united destiny through nationhood.

For Thomas Jefferson love of the world was everything, and things of the spirit were suspect unless controlled by rational powers. As "the St. Paul of American democracy," he joined an enlightenment philosophy of religion with a bourgeois political theory of the state.[35] Religion was to provide a moral tone for the nation, but certainly was not to be a force stronger than the state. No established religion was to be supported by the state, nor was it to support the state. Whereas Roger Williams had earlier sought to separate the church from the state so that the church would not be contaminated by the state, Jefferson sought to separate church and state so that the state would not be contaminated by the church.[36]

The founders assumed a generalized religion (nonestablished) that would pervade the whole purpose of the nation. Their enlightened philosophy of religion (in relation to the state) was that of Deism, which recognized an impersonal force that ruled the universe from long ago and far away. The fathers of the nation (including George Washington, Thomas Paine, John Adams, and Benjamin Franklin, as well as Jefferson) applied Deism to the national purpose. As religious historian Martin E. Marty notes in reference to the acceptance of the Deist tenets: "Some sort of God held people accountable now or later because morality had been implanted as a possibility in people. The nation being born must be responsible and must seek virtue."[37] Deism would serve as the cohesive force for the whole nation; a "religion of reasonableness" would serve as the religion of the United States.

Although the national religion of reasonableness was not theologically compatible with evangelicalism, it did furnish a common link between morality and religion, on the one hand, and national welfare on the other. After the Revolution, Timothy Dwight, the Congregational minister and president of Yale University and the grandson of Jonathan Edwards, could provide a rationale for the inseparability of public morality and religion:

> Morality, as every sober man, who knows anything of the subject discerns with a glance, is merely a branch of Religion; and where there is no religion, there is no morality. Moral obligation has its sole ground in the character and government of God. But, where God is not worshipped, his character will soon be disregarded; and the obligation, founded on it, unfelt, and forgotten. No duty, therefore, to individuals, or to the public, will be realized, or performed. Justice, kindness, and truth, the great hinges on which free Society

hangs, will be unpracticed, because there will be no motives to the practice, or sufficient forces to resist the passions of men. Oaths of office, and of testimony, alike, without the sanctions of religion are merely solemn farces.[38]

Dwight's emphasis on the importance of Christian religion for a public morality was a philosophy that has ideally served as the basis for a Christian nation. That the connection has not always (perhaps rarely) guided actual political conduct says something about either the weakness of the connection or the direction of the religion that underlies a public morality. The secularized religion that must support a capitalist nation is not the religion that can have much positive consequence—other than furnishing a dubious legitimation to the nation. This is to be remembered when we later consider the possibilities of a "civil religion" in the United States.

The secularization of Puritanism in the political as well as economic development of American capitalism thus consisted of molding Puritanism into a myth that would accommodate the various contradictions of developing capitalism. The colonial Puritan emphasis on the theology of the religious covenant became an embodiment of the universal design of the nation.[39] Early New England theology provided a framework for transposing secular interests back into the mold of a sacred theology, albeit a theology that was secularized by the crudest of political and economic values (those shaped by capitalism). A Puritan myth was created in the course of secularization that gave support to developing capitalism. Religion—in its political and economic secularization—had become (in the Marxist sense) ideology. This is indeed the danger of adapting religion to this world, as it most certainly must be adapted to be made relevant to life. But the danger is especially acute and certain when that adaptation is made within a developing *capitalist* society.

Religion is continually used to support the political and economic institutions of the United States. The notion of the United States as the Redeemer Nation has been enlivened with various religious revivals. In order to make this notion palatable, religion has been placed into the already existing ideals and patterns of bourgeois American life. This has happened repeatedly in evangelical Protestantism: "Patriotism, manifest destiny, Anglo-Saxon self-confidence, the common man's social and economic aspirations, peaceful community life, the Declaration of Independence, and the Constitution—all were accommodated and supported in its capacious system of beliefs."[40] There have been important religious dissent movements from the mainstream tradition, dissent from which we can learn much, but the cautionary tale of our history is that religion needs to be carefully attended to when practiced under capitalism. The ideology embodied in this country's official motto—"In God We Trust"—is a real one that has to be confronted in any religious reconstruction of social and moral life in this society.

The secular belief (but sacredly sanctioned) that the United States is the Chosen Nation and a beacon to the rest of the world is, however, an ideology that is fast waning as the twentieth century nears its end. As capitalism reaches its last stages of development, the religious support it has enjoyed can no longer be taken for granted. The belief that providence has assigned a worldly mission to the United States is no longer accepted as the true providence. Longfellow's hymn of the national majesty of the Union has lost its credibility.

> Sail on, O Union, strong and great!
> Humanity with all its fears,
> With all its hopes of future years,
> Is hanging breathless on thy fate![41]

Theologically and existentially, we have lost our trust in the nation. Christian piety must be found and placed elsewhere. The God of Israel has made a judgment. The nation is not (and never was) the instrument of providence.

A RELIGIOUS AWAKENING

It has often been the religious impulse that has led the resistance against the mainstream of developing American capitalism. Even in the colonies there were religious minorities which did not accept the emerging establishment, an establishment that was attempting to merge the economy, the state, and a secularized religion. The Puritans objected to the Anglican establishment; the radical wing of Puritanism, including the Baptists, Quakers, and Roger Williams's separtists, made their own dissent. Such groups as the Dutch Reformed and the Swedish and German Lutherans separated themselves from the mainstream, and much later (in the period of industrial capitalism), a wide range of religious groups made known their objections to the nation and its economy.[42] To be sure, the reactions differed considerably in the nature of the response as well as in what they focused on. But they had in common a critical stance toward the world that was informed by a depth of religious consciousness.

We find an example and an inspiration in Puritanism's religious concern and response. When Puritanism is considered in the broad perspective of Christian history, as Perry Miller observes, "it appears no longer as a unique phenomenon, peculiar to England of the seventeenth century, but as one more instance of a recurrent spiritual answer to interrogations eternally posed by human existence."[43] In spite of adjustments it later made to the developing nation, Puritanism is a religious spirit that is with us always.

As Puritanism developed it became more and more encased in technical jargon and increasingly distracted by economic and social issues; as it waned it partook more of the qualities of one age and became less of a gospel for all time. But as long as it remained alive, its real being was not in its doctrines but behind them; the impetus came from an urgent sense of man's predicament, from a mood so deep that it could never be completely articulated. Inside the shell of its theology and beneath the surface coloring of its political theory, Puritanism was yet another manifestation of a piety to which some men are probably always inclined and which in certain conjunctions appeals irresistibly to large numbers of exceptionally vigorous spirits.[44]

This Augustinian piety of Puritanism, a piety driven by (as Miller notes) a quest for satisfactions that nothing of this earth could ever supply, is relevant to us today. In our search for the prophetic in theology and in life, we draw from Puritanism a desire to be carried across the gulf separating existence from essence. We are guided by the basic belief that disorder of the universes will be righted and that we are brought into harmony with a divine plan. The substance of this Augustinian piety—embodied in Puritanism—is that when knowledge of God is achieved the answer to all other questions will soon follow.[45]

When the essence of this piety—this eternal drive for reconciliation and redemption—is ruptured, threatened or eroded, the spirit seeks to be renewed. As the colonies became increasingly secularized, moving into the early 1700s, there was a Puritan religious response to restore the essence of spiritual piety. The Great Awakening that swept through the colonial commonwealth of North America was a clear religious challenge to the established, secular authority of the developing society. The consequences were diverse and contradictory, ranging from revitalizing Puritan piety to giving further spiritual heritage to an American nation. Among other things, the Great Awakening brought with it a reassessment of the social patterns that were emerging in the New World. Perhaps most important for us, the Great Awakening was a renewal of the dialectic between reason and spirit. It provided a redefinition of the place of the religious spirit in an age of increasing secularity. The religious awakening offers a stance for being in the world but also being apart from it, that is, in it but not always of it.

The first stirrings of the Great Awakening began in the Northampton, Massachusetts, Congregational parish of Solomon Stoddard. His powerful Calvinistic preachings had moved his parishioners in a series of revivals. By 1734, shortly after his grandson Jonathan Edwards had succeeded him, the religious response began to accelerate.[46] The movement quickly spread to the adjoining towns and moved down the Connecticut valley to Saybrook and New Haven. The Great Awakening widened, spreading to other parts of the eastern coast, especially stimulated by the preaching of the English evangelist George Whitefield. The Awakening was becoming a major means for many diverse people to respond to the changing moral, intellectual, and social conditions of the growing commonwealth. The results of these few short years were far-reaching; a form and a substance were created for all future religious revivals in the United States.

For its immediate participants, the Great Awakening meant a confrontation with many diverse and opposing ideas. An historian of the Great Awakening, Edwin Scott Gaustad, observes that "within the lifetime of many of the principals of the Awakening the central issues of an evangelical Christianity—general or particular atonement, a human or divine Christ, reason or revelation, reform or regeneration, free or earned grace—were subjected to severe testing."[47] Among theologians new division arose which expanded upon the Old Light-New Light dichotomy of religious experience. The theological implications of the Awakening were to be struggled with for the next two hundred years of theological development, founding in its wake schools of theology and universities to incorporate these theologies. Paramount was the theology of Jonathan Edwards, a theology that has renewed relevance in our own age where the sacred and secular dialectic is pressing again upon us.

The "New England Theology" that grew from Jonathan Edwards's preaching and theological discourses took shape in large part through the repeated encounters between Edwards of Northampton and Charles Chauncy of Boston. In his book of 1742, *Some Thoughts Concerning the Present Revival of Religion in New England*, Edwards spoke to all the world about the nature of his religion.[48] Representing the enlightenment thought of the Boston liberal community, Chauncy answered in the next year with his own *Seasonable Thoughts of the State of Religion in New England*. He denounced the revival as a resurgence of the antinomian (faith alone being necessary for salvation) and enthusiastic heresies that had plagued the early Puritans. In his conclusion Chauncy stated the chief issue posed by the revival: "There is the Religion of the Understanding and Judgment, and Will, as well as of the Affections; and if little Account is made of the former, while great Stress is laid upon the latter, it can't be but People should run into Disorders."[49] Edwards responded to the challenge in 1746 with his important theological work titled *A Treatise Concerning Religious Affections*. As one of the most profound inquiries into the nature of religious experience, it is a classic evangelical answer to the question, What is true religion?

Edwards's thesis is that true religion springs from and consists of "holy affections." The "affections" are not simply the emotions or the will, but that which inclines the heart to possess or reject something— with love itself being the source of all the affections. Religious experience is thus seen as an organic whole, encompassing all human faculties, but especially that of the deepest emotion inspired by God. In an earlier sermon, "A Divine and Supernatural Light" (published in 1732), Edwards talked about his new spiritual sense of understanding, this sense of the heart. It is a spiritual light, a "true sense of the divine excellency of the things revealed in the word of God, and a conviction of the truth and reality of them thence arising." "Thus there is a difference," Edwards continues, "between having an opinion, that God is holy and gracious, and having a sense of the loveliness and beauty of that holiness and grace. There is a difference between having a rational judgment that honey is sweet, and having a sense of its sweetness." [50]

Hence, the essence of all true religion for Edwards lies in holy love and the light that is the foundation of that love—and all the fruits of this religion. (In the words of II Corinthians 5:17, "Therefore if any man be in Christ, he is a new creature: old things are passed away; behold, all things are become new.") Gaustad concludes his discussions of Edwards by noting that Edwards was a "mystic in an accepted sense of the word, for he was one of that company who believe themselves to have had an experience of God and for whom that experience is the most absolute, certain, and joyful source of knowledge and basis for behavior." [51] Religious experience, as an affection of the heart, shapes our whole being. It is an immediate divine influence, convincing the mind and governing the heart.

The theological differences between Edwards and Chauncy went far beyond the specific debates of the Great Awakening. Their differences were part of the long-established dialectic between piety and enlightenment, between faith and reason. Whereas Chauncy sought truth in common sense and natural philosophy, Edwards sought truth in a revelation revived by religious experience. Gaustad observes: "Augustine's God was also Edwards', and Augustine's 'faith seeking knowledge' is an intellectual biography of his New England counterpart. However much knowledge one searches for and finds, it is with faith that one begins." [52] For Edwards this did not mean ignoring reason; reason was to be used but not to be glorified as the origin of truth and experience.

Piety as the life force of religion in a confrontation with the reason of the intellect is the legacy of the Great Awakening to us today. The awakening continues to be very much with us. Although enlightenment thought tended to reduce religion to an amorphous humanistic morality, and pietism often was reduced to a mindless subjectivity, the dialectic in its purest form persists in our own age. The choice is not, as the history since about 1800 seems to indicate, a choice between one or the other. Faith and reason must be brought together, with all of the dialectic involved. This is the task of a Christian theology—of a theology that is appropriate for an emerging socialist society. The task is not easy—it requires bringing heart and mind together, allowing the ultimate truth to be made worth the seeking. "Of course it is easier not to climb at all, to settle for Greek or Hebrew, science or poetry, mind or matter. But to accept one source of truth to the exclusion of all other sources is to court disaster on a fearfully grand scale. Besides, the climb is exhilarating—or so thought the Puritan."[53]

The piety of Puritanism, the sense of a continual divine awakening, has had its effects on the subsequent religious and intellectual movements in the United States. Some of the same sense of inward communication is found in the transcendental movement of the mid-1800s, although such figures as Ralph Waldo Emerson stripped from Puritanism much of its sacred element, turning instead to the metaphysics of nature.[54] Although the search of evangelical religion for a pure Christianity was the main cultural force of the period, outside of the secularizing spirit of capitalism, transcendentalism was also a response to the increasing industrialization and capitalist rationality. Developing as a protest movement within the Unitarian Church in New England during the 1830s, transcendentalism was a quest for an authentic religious experience, inspired by the Puritan example but rejecting the creeds and rites of Puritanism. An historian of the movement thus writes: "In its sense of joy and wonder at creation and in its deep-seated belief that natural processes possessed unmistakable direction and purpose, American Transcendentalism, for all its heresies, was profoundly religious in temper."[55]

Transcendentalism, however, did not suggest a collective or social struggle against developing capitalism. Although it furnished a critique of the existing order, it was at heart an appeal for moral reform of the individual. Emerson was strongly laissez-faire in his economic views, arguing the necessity of inner guidance in social and political affairs, yet insisting on equality and praising the ideas of the utopian socialists. The vision of the transcendentalists was generally optimistic, however austere. "Like Hegal (and like Marx, too), they believed in cosmic progress; they thought the world was unfolding according to an immanent, necessary, and beneficent plan."[56] With a fresh sense of wonder, the transcendentalists believed that we could move closer to the mystery of creation and thereby be renewed. But this was by now a piety that was devoid of the significant religious symbolism of the Puritans.

Of greater consequence for the renewal of religious awakening—as people moved westward in the nineteenth century—was the evangelical religious movement. On the frontier the churches answered fundamental human needs on the social as well as religious level. The churches (especially Presbyterian, Baptist, and Methodist) were complex institutions that served as centers for spiritual needs and for such social requirements as health, education, counsel, and community.[57] Where there was otherwise a lack of organizations and institutions on the frontier, the church provided sustenance for body and for soul. Similar to the functions provided in New England at an earlier time by the Puritans, the churches of the frontier gave the westward settlers a home. Although more limited now, with further adaptation being made to developing capitalism, the revival religion of the frontier kept alive the spirit of divine redeeming grace.

Yet the secularization of religion, as capitalism continued to develop in the United States, took us further away from the divine spirit. A secularization of religion that aided capitalist development exalted the divine in the "American" and the divine in the capitalist nation and its purpose. The distinctions between human life and God, between finite time and eternity, became obscured. However, some writers (such as Nathaniel Hawthorne), in response to both liberal humanism (including transcendentalism) and the capitalist spirit, continued to insist that as human beings we live both in time and out of it, and that the constant interaction between time and eternity constitutes a necessary part of our tragic (but essential) destiny.[58] Without this realization we become our own messiah; we need to understand instead that as human beings we find completion only in something greater than ourselves. The real basis for any human community lies, the literary critic F. O. Matthiessen warned, "not in humanitarianism but in men's common aspiration and fallibility, in their humility before God."[59]

In spite of a secularized humanistic religion, and in spite of the materialism of capitalism and a material analysis of that materialism, there is no such thing as a purely material and rational world. And the traditional dichotomy between reason and faith only serves to further the tendency to divide and separate our experience into the spiritual realm, on the one hand, and the rational realm on the other. The question, rather, is to what spirit will reason be put. Reason is rooted historically in culture and religion. What is worth knowing reasonably about is guided by our spiritual sense. Human salvation, in the end, is not derived from intelligence nor the rationality of the disciplined mind, but from religious awareness of the divine—infinite and eternal—attended to with all the faculties of our hearts and minds.

NOTES

1. Perry Miller, *The New England Mind: The Seventeenth Century* (Boston: Beacon Press, 1961), p. viii.
2. Ibid., p. 396.
3. Perry Miller, *The New England Mind: From Colony to Province* (Boston: Beacon Press, 1961), p. 15.
4. Page Smith, *As a City Upon a Hill: The Town in American History* (New York: Alfred A. Knopf, 1966), pp. 192–193.
5. Miller, *The New England Mind: From Colony to Province*, pp. 21–22.
6. On this notion of secularization, see Ronald L. Johnstone, *Religion and Soci-*

ety in Interaction: The Sociology of Religion (Englewood Cliffs, N.J.: Prentice-Hall, 1975), pp. 295–299.

7. Herbert Aptheker, *The Colonial Era* (New York: International Publishers, 1966), p. 85, quoting René Descartes.

8. Ibid., p. 86.

9. Ibid., p. 88. Also see Henry R. May, *The Enlightenment in America* (New York: Oxford Press, 1976).

10. Franklin L. Baumer, *Modern European Thought: Continuity and Change in Ideas, 1600–1950* (New York: Macmillan, 1977), p. 141.

11. Ibid., p. 160, quoting Alexander Pope.

12. Ibid., p. 162.

13. Robert Anchor, *The Enlightenment Tradition* (New York: Harper & Row, 1967), p. 8.

14. Baumer, *Modern European Thought*, p. 314.

15. James Luther Adams, *On Being Human Religiously: Selected Essays on Religion and Society*, ed. and intro. Max L. Stackhouse (Boston: Beacon Press, 1976), p. 240.

16. See Eric J. Hobsbawm, "Introduction," in Karl Marx, *Pre-Capitalist Economic Formations*, ed. E. J. Hobsbawm (New York: International Publishers, 1965), pp. 9–65.

17. See Douglas R. McManis, *Colonial New England: A Historical Geography* (New York: Oxford Press, 1975); Edwin C. Rozwenc, *The Making of American Society*, vol. I (Boston: Allyn and Bacon, 1972), pp. 114–121; and William Appleman Williams, *The Contours of American History* (New York: Quadrangle, 1966), pp. 75–148.

18. Hugh Mosley, "The Founding Fathers and the Accumulation of Capital," *Politics and Society*, 6 (No. 1, 1976), pp. 105–116.

19. See Paul M. Sweezy, *The Theory of Capitalist Development* (New York: Monthly Review Press, 1968).

20. Erik Olin Wright, "Alternative Perspectives in the Marxist Theory of Accumulation and Crisis," *The Insurgent Sociologist*, 6 (Fall, 1975), pp. 5–39.

21. See the statistics and economic history presented in Douglas C. North, *The Economic Growth of the United States, 1790–1860* (New York: Norton, 1966); and Douglas C. North, *Growth and Welfare in the American Past: A New Economic History*, 2nd edition (Englewood Cliffs, N.J.: Prentice-Hall, 1966).

22. See Aptheker, *The Colonial Era*, pp. 35–37.

23. James B. Hedges, *The Browns of Providence Plantations: Colonial Years* (Cambridge, Mass.: Harvard University Press, 1952), p. 329. On subsequent developments in Rhode Island, see Peter J. Coleman, *The Transformation of Rhode Island, 1790–1860* (Providence, R.I.: Brown University Press, 1969).

24. Jurgen Kuczynski, *A Short History of Labour Conditions Under Industrial Capitalism in the United States of America, 1789–1946* (New York: Barnes & Noble, 1973), pp. 65–66. Also see Norman Ware, *The Industrial Worker, 1840–1860* (Boston: Houghton Mifflin, 1924).

25. Gary Kulik, "Pawtucket Village and the Strike of 1824: The Origins of Class Conflict in Rhode Island," *Radical History Review*, no. 17 (Spring, 1978), pp. 5–37.

26. Kuczynski, *A Short History of Labour Conditions Under Industrial Capitalism in the United States of America*, pp. 105–122. Also see Gabriel Kolko, *Main Currents in Modern American History* (New York: Harper & Row, 1976), pp. 1–99.

27. Kuczynski, *A Short History of Labour Conditions under Industrial Capitalism*, pp. 171–172.

28. See James O'Connor, *The Fiscal Crisis of the State* (New York: St. Martin's Press, 1973).
29. Smith, *As a City Upon a Hill*, p. 15. Underlining is mine.
30. Robert T. Handy, *A Christian America: Protestant Hopes and Historical Realities* (New York: Oxford Press, 1971), especially pp. 3–6.
31. Miller, *Errand into the Wilderness*, p. 142.
32. Ibid., p. 143.
33. Ibid.
34. Sydney E. Ahlstrom, *A Religious History of the American People* (New Haven: Yale University Press, 1972), pp. 356–359.
35. Ibid., pp. 367–368.
36. Miller, *Errand into the Wilderness*, p. 146.
37. Martin E. Marty, *Religion, Awakening and Revolution* (Gaithersburg, Md.: McGrath Publishing Co., 1977), p. 151.
38. Handy, *A Christian America*, pp. 23–24, quoting Jonathan Edwards.
39. Sacvan Bercovitch, *The Puritan Origins of the American Self* (New Haven: Yale University Press, 1975), especially pp. 136–186.
40. Ahlstrom, *A Religious History of the American People*, p. 805.
41. Ibid., p. 383, quoting Henry Wadsworth Longfellow.
42. See Handy, *A Christian America*, pp. 14–16; and Ahlstrom, *A Religious History of the American People*, pp. 805–124.
43. Miller, *The New England Mind: The Seventeenth Century* p. 4.
44. Ibid.
45. See Ibid., p. 8 for a fuller account of Augustian piety: "The heart of this piety was its sense of the overwhelming anguish to which man is always subject, and its appeal to anguish-torn humanity has always been its promise of comfort and of ultimate triumph. The Augustinian strain of piety flows from man's desire to transcend his imperfect self, to open channels for the influx of an energy which pervades the world, but with which he himself is inadequately supplied. . . . If man once achieved knowledge of God and of his soul, the answer to all other questions would soon follow. The irrepressible demand of the soul for this knowledge is the driving force of the piety."
46. Ahlstrom, *A Religious History of the American People*, pp. 282–294.
47. Edwin Scott Gaustad, *The Great Awakening in New England* (New York: Harper & Row, 1957), p. 126.
48. Ahlstrom, *A Religious History of the American People*, pp. 302–303.
49. Ibid., p. 303, quoting Charles Chauncy.
50. Gaustad, *The Great Awakening in New England*, p. 100, quoting Jonathan Edwards.
51. Ibid., p. 101.
52. Ibid., p. 83.
53. Ibid., p. 140.
54. Miller, *Errand into the Wilderness*, pp. 184–203.
55. Paul F. Boller, Jr., *American Transcendentalism, 1830–1860: An Intellectual Inquiry* (New York: G.P. Putnam's Sons, 1974), p. 32.
56. Ibid., p. 167.
57. T. Scott Miyakawa, *Protestants and Pioneers: Individualism and Conformity on the American Frontier* (Chicago: University of Chicago Press, 1964), especially pp. 3–18 and pp. 213–240.
58. Giles B. Gunn, *F. O. Matthiessen: The Critical Imagination* (Seattle: University of Washington Press, 1975), p. 113.
59. F. O. Matthiessen, *American Renaissance: Art and Expression in the Age of Emerson and Whitman* (New York: Oxford University Press, 1941), p. 446.

4
The Social and Moral Order of Advanced Capitalism

How can we obey Christ's law of love, when every industrial maxim, custom, fact, and principle renders that law inoperative.
GEORGE D. HERRON, "The Social System and the
Christian Conscience," in *The Kingdom*, 1898

The growth of capitalism has meant the increasing division of society into the two opposing classes, between those who own and control the means of production and those who do not, between those who appropriate labor power and those who must sell their labor power. A developing capitalist economy is thus characterized by a growing conflict and struggle between the capitalist class and the working class. At the same time, the problems created by capitalist development must be dealt with in some way by the capitalist system. For capitalism to continue—assuring further capital accumulation and legitimation of the capitalist system—the problems created by its own contradictions have to be regulated and controlled. A system that cannot generate a humane existence, without altering beyond recognition its basic mode of production, responds by attempting to integrate the problems of its own creation into the overall system. Hence, the capitalist state has emerged to manage outside of the private economic sphere the problems of a developing capitalist economy.

Institutional forms within a growing state apparatus have been devised to meet the changing demands of the new industrial capitalism. Between 1880 and 1920 new forms of state control were established for managing the problems brought about by the industrial stage of capitalism.[1] Since that time, as capitalism has moved to an advanced stage of development, the capitalist state has become even more important in regulating capitalist society and its problems. The economic and political structure of advanced capitalism is in the process of transformation, finally reaching the late stage of its development. Within the dialectics of this development is the emergence of social conditions and a class consciousness arising from those conditions for the transformation to a socialist society.

The advanced stage of capitalist development also signifies the end of a social and moral trend that has been accelerating since the beginning of capitalism: the trend toward religious skepticism and indifference. The advanced capitalist society has become the most secular society in the history of the world. Advanced capitalist is also advanced secularism. That developing capitalism and developing secularity have gone hand in hand is due to the internal demands of capitalism. An economy of exploitation requires an areligious ethic or spirit that legitimizes the further development of the economy as well as its present practices.

The sacred religious spirit, however subterranean it may be, has continued in spite of the development of capitalism. And the rise of new theologies and religious movements attests to the persistence of the human need for the sacred. That the sacred must become a part of the world again is the message of a religious socialism. A socialism without the sacred would become a system as materialistic and alienating as capitalism. What is emerging in the transition to socialism is a new religious concern, a concern which not only repudiates the essential secularity of capitalism but also makes socialism whole by integrating it with the sacred.

THE ADVANCED SECULAR SOCIETY

Writing in a Nazi prison in 1944 to a pastor friend, the theologian Dietrich Bonhoeffer outlined the religious landscape of western civilization. Soon to be executed by his persecutors for his role in the German Resistance, Bonhoeffer described in agonizing clarity the all but total secularization of culture. He wrote with pressing concern about the world's "great defection from God," indicating that the secular movement has reached a "certain completion," and that we have "learned to cope with all questions of importance without recourse to God as a working hypothesis." [2] In questions of science, art, and even ethics, the metaphysics of a supreme being or force is rarely considered anymore.

The drift toward secularism, as Bonhoeffer observed, represents the culmination of a movement that began in the Middle Ages. The sources are many and complex in the movement that is finally reaching its completion in our own time. Certainly, the older theistic conceptions could not withstand or be appropriate for the intellectual, political, and economic developments of the subsequent centuries. And in our century, as the intellectual historian Franklin L. Baumer points out, the increasing belief in the relativity of history undermines a belief in any absolute notion of human existence: "History showed everything, law, morality, religion, and art, to be in ceaseless flux." [3] The postwar era has been intellectually and spiritually characterized by a belief in the relativity and transitoriness of all things. The malaise is both a product and a cause of the current tendency to reject or refuse to raise questions of ultimate concern. Whether an interest is lost in religious questions (remaining silent about such questions), or whether the mood is one of despair regarding the ultimate, our age is reaching the final state in a long process of secularization.

The crisis of advanced capitalism is thus both material and spiritual. Materially, capitalism has reached a point in which it cannot advance economically or politically without altering the basic capitalist mode of production. The social problems created by capitalist production can no longer be solved within the framework of capitalism. Moreover, the capitalist state, once a political device for dealing with the economic contradictions of capitalism, is nearing the end of its ability to accommodate the problems of developing capitalism; the capitalist state itself is increasingly subject to contradictions and crises.

Modern welfare state policies, rather than solving the structural contradictions of capitalism, serve to exacerbate the problems and create new ones. The growing surplus population generated by the demands of advanced capitalism cannot be handled by the welfare state. Advanced capitalist society is producing a growing reserve army of the unemployed and unemployable.[4] The modern state has neither the ability nor the financial resources to integrate the displaced and alienated population produced by the capitalist mode of production. More state control and repression become necessary, and resistance to that control increases.[5] The attempt by the capitalist state to control the problems generated by late capitalism is the basis of increased social conflict and political struggle.

The capitalist state cannot continue to maintain its legitimacy as it fails to solve the problems created in the promotion of the capitalist economy. Even its attempts at pacification through social services, on the one hand, and repression, on the other, are doomed to failure both economically and on the level of legitimation. The modern capitalist state, on various levels, is in crisis; and it is a crisis that will continue to increase as long as the capitalist system resists transformation into a socialist system.

The dialectic of class struggle assures a continuing conflict within capitalist society, generating the eventual transformation of capitalism. The capitalist state, in not only failing to eliminate class struggle but, in fact, increasing it, contains the contradictions for its own demise. While the expanding function of the state means more state control, it also means that larger portions of the population become politicized. For the expanding working class of capitalist society, a political consciousness is developing, a consciousness that questions the legitimacy of the existing system.[6] Politically conscious action against the material conditions of capitalism becomes an inevitable part of the class struggle in capitalist society.

Spiritually, capitalism has reached the end of its secular spirit, once characterized by an unquestioning enthusiasm for acquisitiveness and accumulation. Even in this secular realm of spirituality, the majority of the population finds little of the moral and personal support once provided by that spirit. The capitalist world is in disorder, spiritually as well as materially. What is there to believe in when the material world no longer furnishes us with spiritual rewards and sustenance?

In the process of its material development, capitalism has all but destroyed the sacred spirit. Our advanced secular society leaves us without the religious symbolism and belief to be a real part of the world. Without apprehending the infinite and eternal questions beyond this world, we are neither of this world nor any other. We have lost our hold; our qualities have become those of the barren landscape that surrounds us. That we do cope in this world says something about the persistence of the human spirit. That we can rise above the material and secular realm of capitalism attests to the possibilities of God's divine providence in our own life and time.

THE RELIGIOUS RESPONSE TO CAPITALISM

Religious thinking and action, in spite of (or perhaps because of) increasing secularity, continues with renewed emphasis in the late stages of capitalist development. The paradox (or dialectic) is that while capitalist culture has become secularized to the point of ignoring religious questions, religious questions increasingly press upon us. Within theology there continues a debate about how we can talk about God in the present age; and in religion there is a new search for meaning in both the traditional denominations and in the new sects and movements of religious consciousness.[7] At the end of an age of advanced secularism, we seek to make metaphysical statements about God and to fill our own lives with the sacred religious spirit. We are finding meaning religiously in a secular age that is fast nearing its completion. A new religious, ultimate concern is emerging in the transformation of capitalism.

It is the millennial hope of the Judeo-Christian tradition that continues to provide the source for the most critical religious challenge to capitalism. In considerations of this world, the apocalyptic view of redemption is basically a social vision that looks outward at history and society. It is a vision that is fundamentally critical of injustice, oppression, and the suffering produced by an exploitative society. Such a society is totally corrupt; there can be no salvation within it. This is the underpinning of every revolutionary faith. As an observer of the messianic hope has written, "Every movement that preaches the irreformability of the present system and its total corruption, that believes that the only solution is radical overthrow and reconstitution of the world on an entirely new and different basis is apocalyptic in structure, even if it uses social-scientific rather than religious language."[8]

A recovery of the authentic, revolutionary Christian tradition is the force behind the various religious responses to industrial capitalism. The religious movements—and especially Protestant theology—have dealt with the social problems being created by the new industrial capitalism, problems that intensified in the late nineteenth and early twentieth centuries. The "social gospel" movement was the most active form of social Christianity during this period. The social gospel moved modern Christianity toward an explicit religious concern for the society we create. The significance of a *social* gospel is that there can be no individual salvation apart from that of the society as a whole. The struggle against the oppression of capitalist society—toward a socialist society—is a collective struggle. Hence, within the social gospel movement and at times outside of it, a radical social Christianity drew from the various forms of socialism. A Christian socialism emerged in response to developing capitalism—a religious socialism that we continue to build on today.

The social gospel was by no means new to religion in the United States. The major element in the religious heritage of the country was Puritanism, "with its powerfully rooted convictions that the shaping and, if need be, the remaking of society was the Church's concern."[9] The evangelical thrust of the great awakenings served to intensify this tendency. The antislavery movement was in large part stimulated and supported by the social concerns of Christianity. But it was in response to the obvious products and failure of industrial capitalism, shortly after the Civil War, that social Christianity (including the social gospel and Christian Socialism) became a persistent feature of religion in the United States. Not only was social Christianity to shape liberal theology, but it deeply affected a branch of the socialist movement, gave rise to social science (sociology, in particular), became an important part of social action movements (including the civil rights and anti-war movements), and encouraged the present-day "secular theology."

The social element in Christianity, as a historian of the social gospel has noted, is at least as old as the gospel itself.[10] The Hebrew prophets, whose moral aspirations Jesus inherited, were themselves social activists. The followers of Christ have sought to apply his teachings in every age. Moreover:

> The apostolic church experimented with a form of voluntary communism; the Christian ethic wrought a decided change in the mores of the Roman world. The Middle Ages, the Reformation, and modern times have all produced their quota of attempts to establish the kingdom of God. The American social gospel is but one of the latest adjustments of the Christian ethic to the exigencies of history.[11]

From the Puritans in the early American colonies to the social Christians of the Gilded Age of industrial capitalism, one can trace the religious pursuit of God's kingdom.

Questions about the kingdom of God provided the critical edge for social Christians as industrial capitalism progressed into the 1880s. Exploitation of labor proved to be the most pressing issue, for it represented an oppression not fitting a Christian world. Although the social gospel was concerned with a wide range of problems, especially poverty and crime, the central focus was steadily on the problems and rights of labor under capitalism. In 1886, the year of bitter strikes and the Haymarket riot in Chicago, Washington Gladden declared that the condition of the industrial world is a state of war: "And if war is the word, then the efficient combination and organization must not all be on the side of capital; labor must be allowed to make combinations necessary for the protection of its own interests." [12] A recognition of the class struggle engendered by industrial capitalism, and the plight of labor within that struggle, continued to be at the heart of the social gospel.

The class struggle under industrial capitalism was viewed by Walter Rauschenbusch, the leading social gospel minister and writer of the time, as a struggle in God's kingdom involving a continuous conflict with the kingdom of evil. The kingdom comes not by peaceful development; and it knows no final consumption in history. Disclosing his vision of God's coming kingdom in his book *Christianity and the Social Crisis*, Rauschenbusch wrote:

> Perhaps these nineteen centuries of Christian influence have been a long preliminary stage of growth, and now the flower and fruit are almost here. If at this juncture we can rally sufficient religious faith and moral strength to snap the bonds of evil and turn the present unparalleled economic and intellectual resources of humanity to the harmonious development of a true social life, the generations yet unborn will mark this as that great day of the Lord for which the ages waited, and count us blessed for sharing in the apostolate that proclaimed it. [13]

True to the millennial vision, the kingdom of God can never be realized fully in this world. Insofar as it does take place on this earth, it is a kingdom that is always on the way, reaching new heights in the concrete achievements of each generation. [14] The kingdom is for each of us the supreme task and the supreme gift of God. The kingdom is both transcendent and immanent, a dynamic relation of finite life and God's infinite grace.

The demand grew with the social gospel for a technique with which to understand the concrete problems of an industrial-capitalist society. The social gospel movement provided the impetus for religious concern about the earthly kingdom, but more information was needed about society and the temporal reasons for its problems. The social gospel thus began to draw from the emerging social sciences; and, in turn, many social scientists turned their attention to the religious implications of their work. In its beginnings sociology developed as the new "handmaiden" of Christian pastoral theology.[15] Sociology courses were established in seminaries and schools of theology for the training of ministers in a knowledge about the social world within which their ministry was to take place. Such prominent figures in academia as the political economist Richard T. Ely and the sociologist Albion Small gave their disciplines a social gospel perspective. A Christian sociology was practiced in the early years of the emerging social sciences. Only later, with the further advance of capitalism, did the social sciences develop into scientistic reform oriented academic disciplines.

The Christian tradition has always had a socialist emphasis, with the hope of a Christian order based on socialist relations. That a Christian Socialism would become prominent in the general religious response to industrial capitalism is consistent with the long development of Christianity. The solution to the contradictions of capitalism required a combination of social action and religious concern: such was the age-old link between Christianity and socialism. Although Christian Socialism came to mean many things, prescribing a range of practices (from reformist solutions to social revolution), the union of a transcendental religious concern with the daily struggle for a socialist society was a recovery of the essential Christian message.

In the midst of the social gospel movement, by the end of the nineteenth century, Christian Socialism provided a critique of some of the liberal themes of the social gospel response to capitalism. When pursued without a definite socialist emphasis, the social gospel tended to offer liberal reformist solutions within the context of the present capitalist society. The bourgeois orientation of many social gospel leaders predisposed them to accept presently constituted political and economic arrangements; social justice was to be attempted within this framework. Although there were noted exceptions within the movement, James Dombrowski's criticism of the general tendency of the social gospel is to the point: "Instead of frankly recognizing the struggle and throwing in the lot of religious forces with the workers, to give practical ethical direction to the former, social Christianity held aloof from the struggle or else counseled patience and moral suasion."[16]

Among the Christian Socialists at the turn of the century, the Reverend George D. Herron preached and taught about the problems of a Christianity under the structure and social relations of capitalism. The primary task of religion, he wrote, is to revolutionize the economic base of society.[17] The economic structure within which social life and religion are practiced must be changed. That capitalism is to be replaced by socialism is the explicit message of the most radical wing of the social gospel movement. Although the conditions at the end of the nineteenth century in the United States were more conducive to liberal thoughts and actions, there were socialist thinkers (many influenced by the writings of Karl Marx), among them Henry George, Henry D. Lloyd, as well as George D. Herron, who furnished the most critical analysis of capitalism and the most religiously radical solutions to the problems of capitalism.

In addition to all these religious responses to industrial capitalism, there were numerous educational and cultural endeavors. A newspaper, *The Dawn*, as the voice of the Society of Christian Socialism, was published and later succeeded by *The Kingdom*. The churches created organizations for social action, such as The Church Association for the Advancement of the Interests of Labor (CAIL), the Brotherhood of the Kingdom, the Christian Socialist Fellowship, the Church Socialist League, and the Christian Labor Union.[18] With World War I and the attacks on liberal theology by neoorthodoxy in the 1930s, the social gospel of the Christian church went into a temporary eclipse, to be revived again at midcentury.

Social organizations and action programs similar in form and aim to those of the early social gospel have continued into the last part of this century. Social gospel ethic is obvious in the civil rights movement of the 1950s and 1960s (especially in the person of Martin Luther King, Jr.), in the antiwar movement of the 1960s, and in the present struggles against the social injustices of capitalism.[19] A theology of liberation and a religious socialism are today in the tradition of the Judeo-Christian prophetic gospel. A capitalism that has developed into its final advanced stages prompts a religious-socialist response that speaks to the depths of the prophetic tradition and moves us to the creation of the kingdom—all in relation to the divine process of redemption.

For millions of people in the United States, the Social Gospel has brought the message that capitalism uses human beings to make profit rather than to serve the common good, and that it is therefore the antithesis of the Christian society based on mutual service. The historian of Christian Socialism writes, referring to the ideas of George D. Herron: "A business man is no more justified in making profit the final aim of his store, factory, railway, or capital, than Jesus would have been in accumulating profit by the working of miracles"; concluding that "it is not an accident that oppression, exploitation and unemployment are thrown up by the capitalist system, for these evils are a logical result of that system; they are inherent and inevitable."[20] Social justice and a Christian life are impossible under the capitalist system. It is the duty of all religious people to engage in the struggle for a socialist society.

The gospel message of Christianity and socialism is clear, because they seek moral values that are of universal validity. The socialist historian writes:

> Both Christianity and socialism fight for a socialized world in order that a co-operative society may replace a competitive profit-seeking order, freeing men to labor for the common welfare; that material goods may be devoted to the material and cultural development of all the workers rather than to the creation of profits for the few; that a classless world may be established, with no divisive social lines to destroy the spirit of brotherhood which can only operate in a profound manner in a society which approaches an eqalitarian principle; in a word, that the good life may be made available universally and human beings, wherever found, may be assured of opportunity for the fullest development of all latent potentialities.[21]

However, that socialism might take the place of religion in the pursuit of the good life is the point where a sacred theology must necessarily inform a religious socialism. While the kingdom is to be lived in the present world, its redemptive power is in a transcendent divinity. We work for a social salvation on earth, but that salvation is ultimately in the grace of an eternal kingdom of God. We struggle for the transformation to a righteous society, yet that struggle has an eschatalogical meaning and significance. Religious socialism contains a sacred religion, not a secular one, no matter how social it is or how much it is engaged in transforming this world.

The bourgeois principle is only further served in a secularized religion, even if that religion should be a socialist one. A secularized social gospel would merely aggravate the contradictions of capitalist society. Secularization itself comes out of the bourgeois principle; and it can be broken only by the principle of a sacred religious socialism. This is a socialism in the true prophetic sense, a religious socialism which finds redemption in the struggle for a kingdom on earth that is in reference to—has its fullest meaning in—the future and transcendent kingdom of God. Socialism will play a prophetic and creative role in the new situation as it transforms itself religiously into the sacred and the holy. Religious socialism moves at the same time and in the same way toward social revolution and revelation in God's kingdom.

CIVIL RELIGION IN CAPITALIST SOCIETY

As the struggle for a socialist society and a sacred religion continues, a secular religion gives support to the advanced capitalist society. The trend throughout the development of capitalism in the United States has been toward a secularized religion that politically and economically legitimizes the capitalist system. Industrial capitalism, particularly since the 1890s, has ideologically promoted the belief that citizens of the country belong to a national (secular) religion, that the United States is a Christian civilization on its way to victory and perfection.[22] The United States, it is held under this politically secularized "religion," is a righteous nation divinely inspired since its beginnings. A secularized belief in the manifest destiny of the nation has promoted and legitimized the developing capitalist economy and political state. Indications are, however, that the secularization of religion is nearing an end as capitalism reaches its final development.

Among the students and advocates of the secularized religion of capitalism, this religion that is antithetical to transcendent and otherworldly ends is conceptualized as a "civil region." The term "civil religion" actually refers to several aspects of a politicized belief system, including an emphasis on a national religion, a folk religion, a democratic faith, and a Protestant civic piety.[23] The common thought that runs throughout the discussions is that what people believe religiously is a matter of utmost political importance. Most discussions of civil religion imply the hope that this secularized religion will lead the United States on its manifest course—primarily along capitalist lines.

Discussions of civil religion also suggest that religion in some form is essential for the well-ordered, stable (usually capitalist) society. Will Herberg argues, for example, that every society requires a shared religious faith that gives citizens a common set of ideas and values which makes a unified nation possible. As one of the first contemporary writers to raise the question of civil religion, he contends that the American Way of Life is, in fact, the civil religion of the United States:

> It seems to me that a realistic appraisal of the values, ideas, and behavior of the American people leads to the conclusion that Americans, by and large, do have their "common religion" and that that "religion" is the system familiarly known as the American Way of Life. It is the American Way of Life that supplies American society with an "overarching sense of unity" amid conflict. It is the American Way of Life about which Americans are admittedly and unashamedly "intolerant." It is the American Way of Life that provides the framework in terms of which the crucial values of American existence are couched. By every realistic criterion the American Way of Life is the operative faith of the American people.[24]

More than being merely a common denominator, Herberg argues that the American Way of Life is a religion in itself.

Robert N. Bellah presents another argument with many nuances for the presence of a civil religion in the United States. He states that the central idea of civil religion, despite the existence of specific denominations and traditional religious forms, is that there is a prevailing religious substratum in American society. Bellah writes:

Although matters of personal religious belief, worship, and association are considered to be strictly private affairs, there are, at the same time, certain common elements of religious orientation that the great majority of Americans share. These have played a crucial role in the development of American institutions and still provide a religious dimension for the whole fabric of American life, including the political sphere. This public religious dimension is expressed in a set of beliefs, symbols, and rituals that I am calling the American civil religion.[25]

He contends that civil religion is a viable religion, not a sham, with a prophetic dimension that makes possible national self-criticism and renewal and ultimately the creation of a new communal ethic in the nation. Still, at the heart of his civil religion is the notion that the United States is the promised land.

The argument for a civil religion similarly contends that this secularized religion is necessary for the maintenance of democratic society. In this contention is the confusion of many civil religion proponents (Bellah excepted) in assuming that a democratic society necessarily means one based on a capitalist economy, when, in fact, a democratic society under capitalism is impossible. Nevertheless, the founding leaders of the nation, already promoting a secularized religion, made the connection between democracy and capitalism a basic part of the American ideology.

The major observer of the new nation and guiding light of later liberal social theorists, Alexis de Tocqueville, made the connection into a theoretical law of nature. Tocqueville, heir to a tradition in political philosophy that upheld the need for a civil religion but was antagonistic to the Christian faith, wrote and argued at length on the importance of a secularized, national religion for a liberal democracy.[26] Such a religion, indeed, would serve as a "political institution" for the preservation of a democratic society. Traditional Christianity, in its sacred form, had to be drastically modified in order to have a political usefulness in a democratic society, at least in a society that was organized around a developing capitalist mode of production. Since a democracy (under capitalism) stimulated individualism, according to Tocqueville's argument, a common belief system with religious overtones (a civil religion) was necessary for the development of a democratic, capitalist nation.

That we should look today for a moral basis of American society is quite natural, given the continuing crisis in the capitalist system. Since the nation was founded on a prophetic notion of its mission, it is obvious to look at the present state of the union in moral and religion terms. Bellah is correct when he observes in the preface to *The Broken Covenant* that "if our problems are, as I believe them to be, centrally moral and even religious, then the effort to sidestep them with purely technical organization considerations can only worsen them."[27] A renewed social vision is needed, Bellah notes, a vision that explicitly recognizes once again the covenant of the Puritans with God and each other. But whether or not that rebirth should be in terms of the secularized nation and in terms of a secularized civil religion, is the critical issue. What is needed is not so much a religion to save the United States, but a transcendent religion that gives primacy to the kingdom of God. This is a religion with its own public morality that will guide us in our social, economic, and political formations in the earthly kingdoms of the world.

Rather than offering a salvation to the nation, further advancement of a civil religion will only exacerbate the problems that are already produced in the process of secularization. Civil religion and its development are symptoms of the secularization of religion, which itself is a product of developing capitalism. To try to salvage advanced secular society by an advanced civil religion is to treat the illness with a dose of the disease. And to bring to civil religion a socialist vision, as Bellah finally suggests, is to attempt to rehabilitate a religious form that was faulty and irreligious from the beginning. A socialist vision is necessary, but that vision must be linked to the everyday struggle for socialist relations and the struggle for a transcendent religion. A religious socialism is prophetically expectant of the kingdom; and rather than being tied to the nation, its anchor is in the divine. Our hope takes form not as "Americans," but as children of God.

But, in fact, a civil religion is not being willed into existence in the United States. It appears, as Sydney E. Ahlstrom suggests, that civil religion is on the wain or is certainly being questioned. By the late 1960s, the patriotic elements basic to civil religion were being subjected to severe criticism. Loyalty and obedience to constituted authority were seriously questioned and "the old nationalistic rhetoric was widely repudiated as hollow and deceitful."[28] Civil religion may not be ending completely but is more likely reaching a new form in its secular development. Sanitized of its patriotic rhetoric, it will nevertheless attempt to keep people in the nation united in the final stages of capitalist development. Yet, dialectically in struggle, the seeds of a sacred religious response are found in the final secularization of civil religion.

A critique of civil religion still recognizes the fact that no religion— that no religious symbolism—can have any social meaning unless it is embodied in a concrete social context. Certainly the church is the traditional social embodiment of religion as the clear alternative to the civil religion of the state. Herbert Richardson, a theologian critical of civil religion, writes: "The alternative to civil religion is not mere Christian belief or faith in transcendence, but *ecclesiastical Christianity*. This is because mere beliefs and faith in transcendence can be absorbed into a civil cult."[29] In pursuing a religion in the church. outside of the state, we limit the power of the capitalist state over our being and our struggle. Richardson adds that "We, as citizens, affirm that civil religion is *idolatry* and limit the power of the state only when we affirm and act on the basis of alternative allegiances that restrict our participation in its cult and values."[30] There is a clear alternative to civil religion in a capitalist society:

I pledge allegiance	I believe
to the flag	in God
of the United States	the Father almighty
of America	Creator of heaven and earth
and to the Republic	and in Jesus Christ, his only son, our lord
for which it stands:	who was conceived by the Holy Spirit born of the virgin Mary
One Nation	suffered under Pontius Pilate
under God	was crucified, dead, and buried
Indivisible	the third day he rose again from the dead
with Liberty	he ascended into heaven
and Justice	and sits at the right hand of the Father
for all.	from whence he shall come to judge the living and the dead and I believe in the Holy Spirit the Holy Catholic Church the Communion of Saints the Forgiveness of Sins the Resurrection of the Body and the Life Everlasting.[31]

Yet, and necessarily, we seek a public morality, a social morality as beings living collectively in this world. But whether this morality relates to the nation-state, especially when that political unit is based on capitalism, or to some other social formation is the question. That a socially liberating and religiously sacred morality cannot be ultimately established under capitalism is certain from all we know historically, theoretically, and spiritually. It is one thing to conceive of a civil religion in a capitalist society; it is quite another to realize a religious life in a socialist society. The critical issue is between a secular and a sacred religion, on the one hand, and between a religion that is or is not related to the political state, on the other. The prophetic expectation is for a sacred religion that will be realized in the struggle for a socialist society— although the particular relation to the political state within that society is uncertain, and will be known only in the struggle that is religious as well as political and social.

A religious socialism goes sacredly rather than secularly beyond a civil religion. We are beyond the liberal theory of politics and religion. The liberal, secularized political religion (as it has become embodied in most of the civil religion discussions and reality) was aptly criticized by H. Richard Niebuhr in his often quoted sentence from *The Kingdom of God in America*: "A God without wrath brought men without sin into a kingdom without judgment through the ministrations of a Christ without a cross."[32] The only sovereign is God. "Apart from God the whole thing is meaningless and might as well not have been. Apart from God and his forgiveness nationality and even Christianity particularized in a nation become destructive rather than creative."[33]

The liberal approach to politics and religion, to civil religion, is presently and historically a defense against radical, socialist democracy. In Europe and the United States, from the eighteenth century onward, liberalism has been a reactionary response to a revolutionary socialist democracy. Lockean liberalism was as much a defense against radical democracy as it was an attack against traditionalism.[34] Liberalism in the United States has been a substitute political philosophy and practice for any radical impulses fostered by the American revolution or by the radical activities of the workers struggling against the capitalist mode of production. The liberal tradition has been part of the process of a secularizing religion, removing a revolutionary and sacredly socialist religion from the politics of the nation. The emphasis has been on a civil religion that gives support and legitimacy to the liberal, capitalist state. The vision of a New Jerusalem on earth—always in relation to a transcendental kingdom of God—as shared in a religious socialism, is quite different (and revolutionary) from the ideology and reality of a politicized civil religion that supports a secularized capitalist society.

The separation of religion from the state is both a philosophical and an historical phenomenon. Ultimately, as Karl Marx pointed out, the separation between "civil" society and the state is fallacious and will eventually be eliminated.[35] The separation isolates people from the human context that is innately and simultaneously political and civil: the two are actually one. Human life is alienated when human society is divided into separate spheres of the private and the public. The division between civil society and the state represents the tension between the actual and the ideal, between particularistic interests and those that postulate universality. The solution, Marx adds, must be found beyond the state. Human life can achieve universal content only after the framework of the state has disappeared. That is in the future, when the existing political and civil structures have utilized all their potentialities—when capitalism is transformed to socialism, socialism to communism, and communism to the universal community.

Thus, the struggle is for a society that is infused with both the political and the religious. This model diverges sharply from the liberal-capitalist notion of a religion which ideologically and morally legitimizes the state. Civil religion is a secularized religious ideology that is historically specific to the development of capitalism. In the hope of the socialist principle, however, human life is continuously lived in the context of a world that is charged with the presence of God. Our lives will no longer make the artificial distinctions between the moral, the political, the social, and the economic. Of divine origin and reality is the worldly kingdom; and of divine transcendence is the kingdom of God.

SECULAR THEOLOGY AND BEYOND

Whether we like it or not, the modern world has become secularized, and the process of secularization is the spiritual equivalent of advancing capitalism. At the same time, much of theology—once the primary discipline of metaphysical and transcendental concern—has become secularized. Dietrich Bonhoeffer's lament on the passing of "religion as such," as civilization has "come of age," is accompanied by the suggestion that "God is teaching us that we must live without him." [36] It is God who has died, Bonhoeffer states, but it is with the suffering Christ that we live in this world. This fading of metaphysical vision has been carried to completion in the death-of-God theology. [37] A secular theology has emerged in the advanced secular, capitalist age that restricts theology to empirical statements about human life in this world, without faith in transcendent Being. This is a theology that both reflects and contributes to the problems of the secular age. It is, nevertheless, a theology that exposes the contradictions (material and spiritual) of the modern age thus prompting the potentialities which come out of these contradictions, moving beyond a secular theology in a secular age.

The liberal tradition in Western thought has not only inspired the material development of capitalism, but has stimulated the growth of a secular theology and a respect for secularity itself. Bonhoeffer drew from this liberal tradition in his project for a "Christianity without religion." Being immersed in a German liberal education and culture, he attempted to lay the foundations for a secular religious understanding that would be integral to the liberal and secular culture. [38] His life and thought are an affirmation and appreciation of the secular age. His theology provides us with an idea of the extent to which religion (however secularized) may still function meaningfully in a secular society. That we also may be in the process of forming a meaningful religion that goes beyond our secular times toward the emerging post-secular, religious-socialist era was beyond the project of Bonhoeffer and all the other existing secular theologies. We are moving to an age where we will not be limited to the recourses of the autonomous human being in dealing with matters of existence in a "nonreligious" world. The divine purpose—in going beyond the secular age—is for a religious world, where the sacred and secular become one, where human existence is in this world, and at the same time where there is an essence beyond it.

Currently discussions of the role and future of religion in modern society, especially those by sociologists, tend to assume the continuation of a capitalist, secular society. Although there are considerable differences in the arguments, the underlying assumption tends to be that American society (as well as the Western world) will remain basically the same, with perhaps further secularization. The analyses of contemporary religion thus center on such issues as the "privatization" of religion (Thomas Luckmann), a societal as well as civil religion (J. Paul Williams), a continuing pattern of traditional religion (Andrew M. Greeley), the emergence of alternative religions (Charles Y. Glock and Robert N. Bellah), and the continuing need for a transcendental religion (Peter L. Berger).[39] The prognosis in these accounts is that while religion is becoming more flexible in form and content, it will continue to evolve as a force in society and will continue to affect individual life. Yet these accounts and their forecasts fail to consider the development of religion beyond the capitalist, secular order. The conventional question is how may religion function in a secularized capitalist society? The search is for a meaningful religion in the existing capitalist society. However, it is in the evolving socialist order and in the struggle for a socialist society that the creation of the religion for the future is taking place.

To argue for a recovery of the sacred and the transcendental, as I have been doing throughout, is not to suggest that religion must stand outside of culture. On the contrary, I am contending that the transcendental is known only—and can only operate—in the everyday world of human and social life. Even in the most secular of cultures, the sacred can shape and transform our lives, to say nothing about guiding us in our most mundane affairs. But this is quite different from contending—as a secular theology contends—that our daily religion and our theology must also be secular in a secular society. Our theology, instead, is an active sacred theology in contemporary culture, in a secular culture that is becoming more sacred in the struggle for a socialist society.

The traditional religious response to religious secularization and secular theology argues that religion must stand outside of this world. This response is dramatically represented in the "Hartford Appeal," when in 1975 a group of theologians, church leaders, and social critics issued a statement from Hartford Seminary condemning the increasing secularization of religion and theology.[40] They appeal for the return of the transcendent to religion and the church, but they describe a transcendence that stands outside of culture. All action is to be grounded on the truth that is transcendent, and the truth is to be known only through transcendence itself, not through an involvement in the culture. The Hartford Appeal is addressed to some of the real problems of a secular theology, but it disassociates itself from life, and in such disassociation negates the force of religion in human struggle and abdicates the role of religion in transforming human culture. This is a conservative theology in its return to the sacred. I am arguing for, instead, a prophetic theology that is radical in its dialectic between human existence and an essential transcendence.

The conservative response to secularity has been countered by a group of theologians and religious leaders primarily from the Boston area (as members of the Boston Industrial Mission). Representing more than a secular theological response, "The Boston Affirmation" (as the document is called) moves beyond the secular versus sacred debate. The Affirmations relate the transcendent of the sacred to the world of real life concerns. Rather than giving way to the existing world, to a world that would attempt to exclude the sacred, this world is united with the sacred. To deal with contemporary culture and society, with the struggle in this world, is not necessarily to be secular. This world is its fullest when it also attends to sacred considerations. In other words, in such an affirmation, the sacred and secular distinctions begin to lose their meaning.

The Boston Affirmations conclude with a listing of the ways in which the reality of this world is transformed in the presence of God. "The Transforming Reality of God's Reign is Found Today" begins:

> In the struggles of the poor to gain a share
>   of the world's wealth,
> to become creative participants
>   in the common economic life,
> and to move our world toward an
>   economic democracy of equity and
>   accountability.

This ends with:

> And especially in those branches and divisions of the church where the truth is
> spoken in love, where transforming social commitments are
>   nurtured and persons are brought to
>   informed conviction,
> where piety is renewed and recast in concert
>   with the heritage,
> and where such struggles as those here
>   identified are seen as the action of the
>   living God who alone is worshiped.

It is followed by "On These Grounds":

> We cannot stand with those secular cynics and religious spiritualizers who see
> in such witnesses no theology, no eschatalogical urgency, and no Godly promise of judgment.
> In such spiritual blindness, secular or religious, the world as God's creation is
> abandoned,
> Sin rules,
> liberation is frustrated,
> covenant is broken,
> prophecy is stilled,

wisdom is betrayed,
suffering love is transformed into triviality, and the church is transmuted into a
club for self- or transcendental awareness.[41]

The struggle is thus joined for the "future of faith and the common life."
We are all called to this witness.

Struggling in *this* world is not, by definition, secular. "Secular" is
being in this world without a relation to or a concern for the transcendent,
the sacred. In the union of ultimate concern with the daily life of this
world, the conventional secular-sacred dichotomy is surpassed. We live
instead in the realm of the prophetic. Our struggle in the world is made
real and meaningful by its relation to what is beyond the secular world.

A critical, prophetic theology—rather than being either a secular or a
sacred theology—is a theology that is transcendent at the same time that it
is in search of the earthly kingdom. Prophetic theology does not regard
the perfect kingdom as ever being sufficient for salvation, but apprehends
a harmony between the socialist goals of this world and the redemptive
powers of prophetic Christianity. While a sacred theology that would
ignore life is an escape from the struggles of this world, and while a purely
secular theology is devoid of the transcendent (devoid of a recognition of
the true ground of our being), a prophetic theology is a recovery of the
ancient but persistent dialectical union of existence and essence.

Prophetic theology is a radical theology that avoids the "theology of
radical secularity." Prophetic theology does not renounce a theistic ontology and turn to a finitist perspective (as in "post-theistic theology,"
which is the negation of the theological project). Prophetic theology never
loses sight of the infinite and the eternal.[42] Prophetic theology holds that
religion, in the Judeo-Christian biblical tradition, is an essential fact of life
in the struggle for a worldly socialist kingdom. Overcoming the alienation
of secular life in capitalist society—and in the transformation to a socialist
society—does not mean the end of religion or the movement to a secular
humanism grounded solely in finitude. Rather, the end of secular alienation makes the sacred in our lives even more relevant and possible of
realization. We are renewed—however finite we may be in this world—by
being in a purpose that is infinite and eternal.

The human spirit and the social and moral order fulfilled by that spirit
are grounded in a religion of the deepest sense. To be of the religious spirit
is to be at one with the transcendent and the finite—beyond the finite
world as well as in it. Religion in the deepest sense—beyond sacred and
secular division—is present in all functions of the spiritual life.

We have been taught, however, in our secularized capitalist age to
separate this world from the transcendent. The separation—which continues to give support to the final development of capitalism, while dialectically moving us to union—seeks to divide our lives into secular and

sacred realms. Because of the tragic estrangement of our lives from the essential unity of life and the transcendent, we have become separated from our true being. Paul Tillich has posed for us the problem and the reconciliation in prophetic terms: "According to the visionary who has written the last book of the Bible, there will be no temple in the heavenly Jerusalem, for God will be all in all. There will be no secular realm, and for this very reason there will be no religious realm." [43] Religion will once again become the essential and all-encompassing ground of our being. The separation between the sacred and the secular is healed as we struggle for a socialist culture.

NOTES

1. Gabriel Kolko, *Main Currents in Modern American History* (New York: Harper & Row, 1976), pp. 1–33. On the nature of the state under advanced capitalism, see James O'Connor, *The Fiscal Crisis of the State* (New York: St. Martin's Press, 1973).
2. Dietrich Bonhoeffer, *Letters and Papers from Prison*, ed. Eberhard Bethge (New York: Macmillan, 1966), pp. 194–195. Quoted in Franklin L. Baumer, *Modern European Thought: Continuity and Change in Ideas, 1600–1950* (New York: Macmillan, 1977), p. 439
3. Ibid., p. 443.
4. Claus Offe, "Advanced Capitalism and the Welfare State," Politics and Society, 2 (Summer, 1972), pp. 479–488.
5. See Richard Quinney, *Class, State, and Crime: On the Theory and Practice of Criminal Justice* (New York: Longman, 1977), especially pp. 63–105.
6. Jurgen Habermas, *Legitimation Crisis* (Boston: Beacon Press, 1975).
7. See, in particular, Harvey Cox, *The Seduction of the Spirit: The Use and Misuse of People's Religion* (New York: Simon and Schuster, 1973); and Charles Y. Glock and Robert N. Bellah (eds.), *The New Religious Consciousness* (Berkeley: University of California Press, 1976).
8. Rosemary Radford Ruether, *The Radical Kingdom: The Western Experience of Messianic Hope* (New York: Harper & Row, 1970), pp. 9–10.
9. Sydney E. Ahlstrom, *A Religious History of the American People* (New Haven: Yale University Press, 1972), p. 787.
10. Charles Howard Hopkins, *The Rise of the Social Gospel in American Protestantism, 1865–1915* (New Haven: Yale University Press, 1940), p. 3.
11. Ibid.
12. Robert T. Handy, *A Christian America: Protestant Hopes and Historical Realities* New York: Oxford University Press, 1971), p. 159, quoting Washington Gladden.
13. Walter Rauschenbusch, *Christianity and the Social Crisis* (New York: Macmillan, 1907), p. 422
14. See Ruether, *The Radical Kingdom*, pp. 84–86.
15. See Hopkins, *The Rise of the Social Gospel in American Protestantism*, pp. 149–170
16. James Dombrowski, *The Early Days of Christian Socialism in America* (New York: Columbia University Press, 1936), p. 28.

17. George D. Herron, "The Social System and the Christian Conscience," *The Kingdom*, August 18, 1898, as cited in Ibid., pp. 29–30.
18. See Ruether, *The Radical Kingdom*, pp. 75–91; and Dombrowski, *The Early Days of Christian Socialism in America*, pp. 75–83.
19. See Paul A. Carter, *The Decline and Revival of the Social Gospel: Social and Political Liberalism in American Protestant Churches, 1920–1940* (Ithaca, N.Y.: Cornell University Press, 1954); and Ronald C. White, Jr. and C. Howard Hopkins, *The Social Gospel: Religion and Reform in Changing America* (Philadelphia: Temple University Press, 1976).
20. Dombrowski, *The Early Days of Christian Socialism in America*, p. 187.
21. Ibid., pp. 189–190.
22. Handy, *A Christian America*, pp. 114–115.
23. Donald G. Jones and Russell E. Richey, "The Civil Religion Debate," in Russell E. Richey and Donald G. Jones (eds.), *American Civil Religion* (New York: Harper & Row, 1974), pp. 14–18. Also see Martin E. Marty, *A Nation of Behavers* (Chicago: University of Chicago Press, 1976), pp. 180–203.
24. Will Herberg, *Protestant, Catholic, Jew* (Garden City, N.Y.: Doubleday, 1955), p. 88.
25. Robert N. Bellah, "Civil Religion in America," in William G. McLoughlin and Robert N. Bellah (eds.) *Religion in America* (Boston: Houghton Mifflin, 1968), pp. 5–6.
26. See Sanford Kessler, "Tocquevillle on Civil Religion and Liberal Democracy," *Journal of Politics*, 39 (February, 1977), pp. 119–146; and Norman A. Graebner, "Christianity and Democracy: Tocqueville's Views of Religion in America," *Journal of Religion*, 56 (July, 1976), pp. 263–273.
27. Robert N. Bellah, *The Broken Covenant: American Civil Religion in Time of Trial* (New York: Seabury Press, 1975), p. ix.
28. Ahlstrom, *A Religious History of the American People*, p. 1085.
29. Herbert Richardson, "Civil Religion in Theological Perspective," in Richey and Jones (eds.), *American Civil Religion*, p. 182.
30. Ibid.
31. Ibid.
32. H. Richard Niebuhr, *The Kingdom of God in America* (New York: Harper & Row, 1937), p. 139.
33. Ibid. See Jerry A Irish, "America and the Kingdom of God," *Journal of Religion*, 56 (July, 1976), pp. 238–254.
34. Sheldon S. Wolin, *Politics and Vision: Continuity and Innovation in Western Political Thought* (Boston: Little, Brown, 1960), p. 294.
35. See Shlomo Avineri, *The Social and Political Thought of Karl Marx* (London: Cambridge University Press, 1968), pp. 17–22, pp. 202–220.
36. Bonhoeffer, *Letters and Papers from Prison*, p. 219. See Baumer, *Modern European Thought*, pp. 454–455.
37. See in particular, John A. T. Robinson, *Honest to God* (Philadelphia: Westminster Press, 1963).
38. See James W. Woelfel, *Bonhoeffer's Theology: Classical and Revolutionary* (Nashville, Tenn.: Abingdon Press, 1970), pp. 19, 23.
39. Thomas Luckman, *The Invisible Religion* (New York: Macmillan, 1967); J. Paul Williams, *What Americans Believe and How They Worship* (New York: Harper & Row, 1969); Andrew M. Greeley, *Religion in the Year 2000* (New York: Sheed and Ward, 1969); Glock and Bellah (eds.), *The New Religious Consciousness*; Peter L. Berger, *A Rumor of Angels* (Garden City, N.Y.: Doubleday, 1970).

40. See Peter L. Berger and Richard John Neuhaus (eds.), *Against the World for the World* (New York: Seabury Press, 1976).
41. The Boston Industrial Mission, "The Boston Affirmations," Cambridge, Mass., January 6, 1976, pp. 12–14.
42. A radically secular theology is presented in Thomas Dean, *Post-Theistic Thinking: The Marxist-Christian Dialogue in Radical Perspective* (Philadelphia: Temple University Press, 1975).
43. Paul Tillich, *Theology of Culture* (New York: Oxford University Press, 1959), p. 8.

5
Socialist Culture: Theological Considerations

There remains a boundary for human activity which is no longer a boundary be-
tween two possibilities but rather a limit set on everything finite by that which
transcends all human possibilities, the Eternal. In its presence, even the very
center of our being is only a boundary and our highest level of accomplishment is
fragmentary.

PAUL TILLICH, *On the Boundary,* 1966

The revolution that is socialist and the reformation that is religious continue. We are in the struggle for a religious socialist culture, a culture that joins the realms of finite existence and eternal essence. The historical roots of the struggle are in the prophetic Judeo-Christian tradition. In the prophetic element of socialism we are conscious of the decisive character of our development.

In the emerging socialist culture we are aware of and motivated by the transcendent nature of the religious and prophetic principle. Religious socialism goes beyond the materialist interpretation of existence; it "aims to correct the false anthropology of Marxism and to overcome its heteronomous and utopian impulses by the achievement of an autonomy deepened by theonomy."[1] The religious-socialist principle indicates the way out of the present capitalist and secular era by combining the elements that have been obscured by the era. The demand is not only for a new economic system but for a total integration of our lives with the true ground of our being. On this basis, "religious socialism would overcome the fear, the insecurity, the loneliness, the thingification of the masses of men; in such a way it would overcome the contradictions of our disintegrating world."[2]

Rooted deeply in the prophetic religious tradition is the drive for justice in human affairs. This impulse becomes the divine will operating in history, providing the source of inspiration to all prophets and revolutionaries.[3] The identification of religion and political economy is in the Hebrew prophets who looked upon all history as the divine law in human life. The highly ethical religion of the Old Testament prophets and the New Testament Jesus sees human society from the perspective of a holy and just God who forgives human beings but also judges them. The prophetic soul is hopeful and optimistic in the "confidence that God will form a better society out of the ashes of the present world."[4] The future in this world is built on the prophetic impulse that necessarily transcends this world.

The prophetic is both historical and transhistorical; its transhistorical element shapes the historical, and the transhistorical is fragmented beyond the historical. As Paul Tillich has reminded us, human history is not bound completely by time. The human situation, including human history, is viewed prophetically from a stance between time and eternity.

> It perceives the infinite dignity of the individual person which follows from his relation to eternity. It perceives the boundary of everything human in space and time under the conditions of finitude and guilt. And it poses the question concerning a reconciliation in which the temporal is elevated into the eternal and the eternal becomes effective in the realm of time.[5]

The possibilities of life are neither exclusively economic nor political, but also religious. While the socialist struggle is necessarily temporal and in this world, the expectant goal of religious socialism is transhistorical and eternal.

THE RELIGIOUS BASIS OF MORALITY

Not only have our spiritual lives been made conditional under capitalism with its related secularity, but the everyday morality of our social lives has become separated from the unconditional source. Our whole being tends to be dictated by historically specific goals and demands, tied to the particular interests of capitalism. No wonder, then, that the social and moral order of contemporary capitalist society is corrupt. The social and moral problems of today are a result of the historical nexus of capitalist development and the secularization of religion.

There also has been a steady capitulation of religion to capitalism. A religion that is gradually removed from the unconditional questions and answers of our lives and the universe and that is tied instead to the thoughts conditioned by the present age becomes a decadent force in modern life. Religious life becomes as alienated as the political, social, and economic life of the society. Religious life is transformed into that which fits into the alienated culture of capitalism. Even in much of religious revival, as Erich Fromm has noted, "the belief in God has been transformed into a psychological device to make one better fitted for the competitive struggle."[6] Just as we and our labor become commodities under capitalism, religion and our worship of God tend to be treated as commodities in the everyday marketplace of life. The struggle to be whole again—the struggle to reconcile our existence with our essential nature—

therefore involves a transformation that is both existential (in this world) and transcendent. Social and religious life are inherently inseparable.

A religion that once helped to shape culture has come to be a tool of the culture of advanced capitalism. Religion has to a large extent become bound within capitalist culture. James Luther Adams writes the following about much of contemporary religion:

> It has lost its relatedness to an ultimate ground and aim, and thus has lost much of its original prophetic power. Its God has become domesticated; it is a bourgeois god. In its major effect its ethics are largely indistinguishable from the "ethics" of the bourgeois principle.[7]

As a consequence, religion mainly aggravates the contradictions of capitalist society. Through its emphasis on economic and spiritual individualism and its class-bound moralism, religion (as embodied especially in Protestant Christianity) has become a cause as well as a symptom of the crisis of contemporary capitalist society. If Christianity is to play a prophetic and creative role in its own transformation and in the transformation of capitalist culture, it must effect a profound break with the bourgeois principle. Thus, there is the necessity today of the transformation to a religious socialism.

The transformation is to be grounded in the unconditioned for all that exists conditionally. Through faith in the unconditional ground of our being, we and the world are transformed. To be religious is to be unconditionally concerned, although religion is realized conditionally in culture within history. "History in all its spheres is the arena of salvation, the realm in which the demands of the unconditional are confronted. Salvation occurs in time and through community, in the overcoming of the demonic powers that subvert both personal and social life."[8] Although the prophetic power is unconditionally grounded, it is realized in the construction of the social and moral order of our conditional existence.

Yet, to reduce religion—and the social and moral order that rests on that religion—to the strict imperative of conditional existence is the method of the secularized mind. In that secularized version of belief known as humanism, religion is reduced completely to the conditional. The Judeo-Christian trust in providence is thereby transformed "into a reliance upon a pre-established harmony in the cosmos, in the human psyche, and in society."[9] In humanism the social and moral order are grounded merely on the pursuit of economic and self-interests, according to the conditioned conscience. The conditional nature of secularized belief is concisely stated in the "Humanist Manifesto II," formulated and distributed in 1973. After observing that religion "may inspire dedication to the highest ethical ideals," the Manifesto reads:

We believe, however, that traditional dogmatic or authoritarian religions that place revelation, god, ritual, or creed above human needs and experience do a disservice to the human species. Any account of nature should pass the tests of scientific evidence, in our judgment, the dogmas and myths of traditional religions do not do so. Even at this late date in human history, certain elementary facts based upon the critical use of scientific reason have to be restated. We find insufficient evidence for belief in the existence of a supernatural; it is either meaningless or irrelevant to the question of the survival and fulfillment of the human race. As non-thesists, we begin with humans not God, nature not deity. Nature may indeed be broader and deeper than we now know; any new discoveries, however, will but enlarge our knowledge of the natural.[10]

To this, in the section on "Religion," the Manifesto adds: "We can discover no divine purpose or providence for the human species. While there is much that we do not know, humans are responsible for what we are or will become. No deity will save us; we must save ourselves."[11]

Regarding the grounds for morality, Humanist Manifesto II is clear: "We affirm that moral values derive their source from human experience. Ethics is *autonomous* and *situational*, needing no theology or ideological sanction. Ethics stems from human need and interest."[12] Happiness and the realization of human needs and desires are the continuous themes of humanism. The good life is (or can be) here and now. With reason and intelligence, and individual self-actualization, society is created and social harmony is established. Belief—if there be any need for it—serves the pragmatic function of smoothing social interaction. The social and moral order is grounded completely in the conditional reality of this world.

The reduction of religion to the conditioned demands of social life is also the method of the social sciences. Moreover, the reduction of religion by the social sciences is a reduction to the social and moral demands of a particular society—to capitalist society. Nevertheless, the continuing problem for the contemporary social scientist who is still interested in the moral life of society (if for no other reason than morality provides order and stability) is that of finding the ground for a morality. With a few emerging exceptions, the method of sociologists is to find a grounding for morality in the demands of the existing capitalist society.[13] Any consideration of religious life and the grounding of morality in religion is in the reduction of religious belief to a figment of social and cultural experience. It is clearly implied that religion is an illusion, but a necessary one that gives coherence to a society.

So much for finding a truly religious basis for moral and social order in social science as conventionally practiced. The search for irreducible universals and for the unconditional in religion, however, is the project of a prophetic criticism that must necessarily inform the attempt by social scientists to find a transcendent basis for morality, a religious basis for the social and moral order of society. Within every culture are the signs of the transcendent, operating especially in the social and moral order.

The idea that moral principles are categorical or unconditional in form goes beyond the *moralism* that characterizes any moral consideration in secular society. Moralism is the contemporary attitude, a negative attitude toward life that is a distortion of the moral imperative.[14] Moralism is an oppressive demand that is without grounding in anything beyond itself, other than perhaps an archaic culture. *Morality,* on the other hand, is conscious of its historical roots and is grounded in a transcendent principle that gives religious meaning to the moral act. Without this grounding, the moral act is completely secular and lacking in grace.

The prophetic message of Christianity, as Tillich notes, is that a new reality has appeared with the coming of Christ, "a power of being in which we can participate, and out of which true thought and action can follow, however fragmentarily."[15] It is in the self-transcendent religious spirit that we are grounded in what is ultimate and unconditioned in being and meaning.

The moral imperative, in this grounding, is thus "the demand to become actually what one is essentially and therefore potentially," the true being becoming the actual being within the worldly community.[16] The moral imperative is religious in its unconditional character. In following the moral imperative, we are grounded in an ultimate concern by that which is taken unconditionally seriously. Morality, beyond secular ethics and any concrete religion, is religious in its very essence.

A morality without a religious grounding is one that does not affirm our essential prophetic being. An "autonomous morality" is incapable of ascertaining our essential nature—and of deriving moral principles therefrom—because of our separation from essential being, because of our fallen state.[17] Such a morality is mistaken, false, and ill-conceived; it is a shallow and conditional morality. Thus, there is the need today in the reconciliation that is both existential and transcendent (worldly revolutionary and sacredly religious) for a theonomous morality, a morality grounded in the religious spirit. No matter how much the contents of the socialist morality are conditioned by the current situation, the general moral imperative in our reconstruction is unconditionally grounded. The conditioned character of concrete historical morality does not contradict the unconditional validity of the moral imperative itself.[18] To establish the reunion of our essential nature with our actual nature—socially and personally—is the purpose of a religiously based socialist morality.

CHRISTIANITY AND MARXISM

The search for a religiously based socialism and the general recognition of the need for a religious foundation have been shaped in recent years by an increasing concern about the future of contemporary cultures. The impetus for this concern is brought about by several historical events, including the increasing development of science and technology, the emergence of the Third World's newly decolonized nations, the development of socialism in many nations, and the internal political developments within both communist and capitalist nations.[19] In relation to these concrete developments a "Marxist-Christian dialogue" has emerged that is addressed not only to the future of the world but also to the necessity of forming an alliance between Marxism and Christianity in assuring a future. The dialogue and dialectic are given concrete form in the liberation struggles, especially in Latin American countries.

The growing alliance between Marxism and Christianity rests on theoretical and practical similarities that both have always shared. Within both Christianity and Marxism there is the eschatological imperative on the direction of the future. In its universal messianism and its inclusive eschatology, Christianity "becomes the religious expression *par excellence* of the hope-laden dissatisfaction which spurs man on towards the future."[20] The eschatological imperative is also the underlying project of Marxism, although in Marxism the eschatology is entirely secular. Thus Marxism has opened the door to a worldly transcendence, with the future embodying the essential nature of human existence.

The eschatological convergence of Marxism and Christianity, aside from the sacred-secular difference in the matter of transcendence, is evident in the writings of the Marxist philosopher Ernst Bloch, who influenced later German theologians in formulating a theology of hope. Bloch wrote of the similarities between socialism and Christianity in the following way:

> Socialism and Christianity have many kinds of concordance, especially in the most important matters. It is good that it is so, both in order to give depth to the avowal of socialism as well as—and perhaps even more important—to give the avowal of Christianity a sign of genuineness, and in such a manner that a new era of Christianity will be indicated, one which will light the way as the light of hope: a new era in which the kingdom of the Son of Man will occur not merely as something "above." If the salvation in the Gospel is to become "flesh"—for us or for the men following—there must not be merely something above, but also something before us.[21]

Although the alliance between Marxism and Christianity is continually developing in the struggle for a socialist future, the difference between a worldly transcendence and an absolute transcendence remains a dialectical issue. The Christian notion of the transcendent God and an absolute future gives a profound meaning to the human struggle for a worldly kingdom.

The Marxist-Christian debate that is continuing today draws from a long tradition of Christian-socialist dialogue and practice. On the Christian side, there is the continuous tradition of Christian socialism, which has been in large part a response to developing capitalism in the Western nations. Focusing on the dehumanization of industrial capitalism and on the hope for a world of democratic socialism, Christian socialism has sought to return to its Christian foundations.[22] In Europe and the United States, Christian socialists have adapted Marxism to a Christian understanding of capitalist society and have engaged in a practice for a socialist future.

On the Marxist side, there is a tradition that finds Christian sources in revolutionary action. Frederick Engels, for example, found a radical Christian tradition in the early working class movements. The Marxist Herbert Aptheker, in the United States, has pointed out that early Christianity was revolutionary in itself: "Early Christianity, as befits its revolutionary character and composition, denounced the ruling gods and so was called atheist, excoriated the secular powers and so was called seditious, upbraided the rich and so was called deluded, pointed to private property and the accumulation of profit and its twin, covetousness, as the chief source of evil and so was called a dangerous madness to be extirpated from the earth."[23] The Marxism that we know today developed out of the Judeo-Christian heritage in Germany with its beginnings in left wing Hegelianism and Feuerbach's theological radicalism. The contemporary alliance and dialectic between Marxism and Christianity is in the long tradition that has found the need to integrate religion and socialism to achieve a religiously based socialism and a socialist-based religion.

The Marxist-Christian dialogue is forcing both Marxists and Christians to open themselves and their ideas to reinterpretation and to renew themselves in the struggle for a new kingdom. On the practical level, Christians and Marxists are forming a world wide network known as "Christians for Socialism." The movement began in Chile, where there is a history of a socially oriented Catholic church and a recognition among priests and nuns that only a socialist society will help their poor and working class parishoners. An inter-American assembly, composed largely of clergy and Catholic activists, gathered in Chile in May 1972 and formed Christians for Socialism. The assembly endorsed what is called "a strategic alliance with Marxists for the purpose of achieving socialism throughout Latin America," adding the resolution that "socialism appears to be the only acceptable alternative for bringing an end to the exploitation of class society."[24] The assembly called for revolutionary action by the working class as well as for a critical theory of capitalism. Christians for Socialism continues as an ecumenical movement with a worldwide affiliation of local groups. Religion is a force for socialist revolution, and socialist revolution is a force that is shaping religion.

At the same time that a worldwide movement for a praxis of Christianity and socialism is taking place, Christian theology is increasingly involved in the Marxist-Christian dialogue. As the theologian Thomas W.

Ogletree has suggested in a symposium on the topic, "If we are interested in improving the conditions of human life, we have got to identify and ally ourselves with social forces capable of breaking open an unjust and oppressive situation so that some new possibilities can be brought into being."[25] Referring to the kinds of hope that are inspired by both religion and Marxism, he argues:

> My contention is that we need both levels of hope in order to be realistic—the ultimate religious hope and the concrete historical hope. The Marxists have provided us with a model for giving social reality and substance to the concrete historical expressions of hope. But this level of hope cannot in my judgement legitimately abolish the human significance of a more ultimate level of hope.[26]

It is exactly on this point—the distinction between the secular, concrete, historical hope, on the one hand, and the transcendent, ultimate hope, on the other—that the Marxist and Christian positions in the dialogue become sharply dialectical. Aptheker illustrates the Marxists (secular) position in his response to Ogletree:

> I know that the problem of ultimate hope (salvation) exists, but I do not deal with it as a live option. Of course, we do find in the history of Christianity the two-fold Christian concept of hope that Mr. Ogletree put forth. However, the Marxist rejects this view. Marxism is atheistic.[27]

And Marxism is atheistic, Aptheker argues, because Marxism is scientific and insists on empirical reality and empirical proof. He also offers the standard materialist, but also humanist, argument that religion denigrates the human being.

However, the Marxist position on religion, as illustrated in the Aptheker-Ogletree debate, is far from being concluded. Marxism is a dynamic philosophy and practice that is constantly being shaped and reformulated in the course of human struggle. Aptheker's statement in defense of atheism in Marxism is currently being revised among Marxists. Although he states that "according to the materialist view of the problem of causation, consciousness does not precede reality," and that "this position is fundamental to Marxism and absolutely basic to its program of determining what is wrong in society and how to correct it," more recent Marxist formulations consider the dialectic that takes place between the material substructure and the nonmaterial superstructure.[28] The more progressive conception of the relationship is incorporated in a conception proposed some time ago by Tillich: "The economic sphere is itself a complex sphere, to which all other spheres essentially contribute, so that they cannot be derived from it, although they never can be separated from it."[29] Religion certainly cannot be rejected out of a contention that as part of the superstructure it is unimportant; religion is part of the nonmaterial consciousness that shapes the objective conditions of history. There is no need, moralistically or scientifically, to be an atheist in order to be a Marxist.

Marxist humanism, however, has traditionally excluded the religiously transcendent from its analysis and practice. Although Marxism does not necessarily begin from a theoretical atheism, its secular position is a logical consequence of a humanism that exalts "man" to supreme importance and denies the existence of any reality that might transcend the human being. If God is considered at all, it is God as merely a false projection of our own unconditionality onto a fictitious supernatural being. Marxist atheism, in other words, is basically humanist in origin and scope—grounded in the belief in human autonomy.[30] As a consequence of this affirmation, Marxism is secular and confined to human transcendence without a transcendent God. Marxist atheism is not an end in itself, however, but is a result of its exclusive emphasis on a secular humanism.

Marxist humanism is also reluctant to consider the religious element in human life because of the past history of the alienating influence of religion (mainly institutional religion). Since religion might hinder subsequent human liberation, the sacredly transcendent tends to be rejected as an obstacle. Aptheker writes:

> Human beings make themselves and God, too; the making of God reflects humanity's alienation in a world and a society still unknown and significantly defective. For Marxism, not only is it true that nothing human is alien; it is also true that nothing higher than humanity exists. It is to overcome, as Marx said, all of humanity's limitations, all of its humiliations, all indignities and inadequacies that Marxism exists. No intermediary or intercessor is required; if one were required it would dethrone humanity, demean man, and make impossible *his own* liberation. Anything other than his own is not liberation but mysticism. His own liberation is desired, by himself and for himself and here on earth. For this God is more than an irrelevancy; He is an obstacle.[31]

Thus, Marxist humanism has confined itself to a secular eschatology, believing in the future elimination of the disparity between human existence and a this-worldly essence.[32] The final judgment, accordingly, is in history.

The Marxism in the Marxist-Christian debate, I am arguing, is to be challenged on the wholly secular assumption. In a dialectic between the sacred and the secular, we can recognize the necessity of the religiously transcendent in a Christian Marxism. Without limiting God to an image of a concrete "being," the ground for all our being can be—must be—an integral part of Marxism.

At the present moment in the dialectic, Marxists need to learn about transcendence and Christians need to learn about revolutionary practice.

Instead of limiting the debate solely to questions about the finite versus the infinite, the dialectic of Marxism and Christianity can be fulfilled in the critical and prophetic theology that emerges in relation to concrete practice.[33] Atheism, or complete insistence on a secular humanism, is not in itself an innate presupposition of Marxism; and avoidance of revolutionary involvement in the secular world certainly is not a necessary or historical characteristic of Christianity. Moreover:

> There is an imperative on Christian theology to deal seriously with these atheistic objections, and to work toward the enunciation of a doctrine of God which supports the creative and free initiative of man. Specifically, this leads us to a consideration of the question of transcendence, for it is here that the greatest problem as well as the greatest hope exists for a mutual and constructive understanding between Christians and Marxists.[34]

The purpose of religion is to change the world in anticipation of the Kingdom of God.

The dialectic in the Marxist-Christian debate continues as long as Marxist humanism excludes the transcendent. The dialectic ceases and an integration of Marxism and Christianity takes place when the secular eschatology of Marxism becomes a sacred eschatology as well. The integration is entirely plausible in so far as Marxism has its eschatological roots in the Judeo-Christian tradition. As Adams has observed, "Marx's humanism—his intention to promote the full realization of the potentialities of humanity—cannot be viewed as something completely unique that bears no positive relation to the previous Judeo-Christian humanism."[35] The materialism of Marxism, rather than being the opposite of Christianity, incorporates the central doctrine of Christianity that is committed to the significance of the historical process. Christianity brings to us the importance of the divine in this process, the destiny of humanity being in time and place, through history, but ultimately transcending it.

The faith of a Christian Marxism (or a Marxist Christianity) is grounded both in history and in the grace of its transcendence. The ideal of human fulfillment, in the struggle between justice and injustice, is the universal value shared by Marxism and Christianity. And, we must be certain to note, there are other religions and religious-political movements in the world that also share this vision. Marxism and Christianity are expressions of a universal truth that points toward a redemption to which we all aspire. As Shepherd Bliss, a participant in the theology of liberation, writes: "The problem is not whether we are Christians or Marxists, but whether—as Christians, Marxists, or whatever—our lives point beyond themselves and are united with others struggling for justice."[36] The radical immanence of Marxism and the transcendent power of Christianity are integral parts of an infinite design of divine providence—realized in and through our human history.

A RELIGIOUS SOCIALIST ORDER

The universal expressions that are both religious and socialist continue as always, to be manifested in human history. The communal-religious movements and the Christian socialism of the present century are concrete manifestations of that universal truth that joins immanent social life with the transcendent symbolism and power of religion. In our own age, the secular humanism of Marxist theory and practice and the religious humanism of Christianity combined in the pre-World War II movement known as religious socialism. Although the movement was halted in its development by the war and subsequent postwar events, including the breaking apart (through emigration) of the movement's leaders and the socialist developments in response to the cold war, the idea remains universally alive. Religious socialism is coming back into public consciousness, especially with the recently translated work of Paul Tillich (originally published in Germany in 1933 as Hitler was coming to power—and then suppressed), *The Socialist Decision*.[37] Marxists and Christians alike are again aware of their common heritage and future course.

In the broadest of terms, religion and socialism are brought together by the basic dynamic of the sacred and the secular, by the integration of religion and culture. It is religion, as ultimate concern, which gives meaning to the substance of culture; and culture is the totality of forms in which the basic concern of religion expresses itself.[38] Every religious act is culturally formed, and the content of every cultural form is an expression of religion in its deepest sense. Religion on this earth, the only religion that we can know, is known through our culture as it historically develops. Religious socialism thus represents in our own time the essential unity of religion and culture. The transcendent is realized through and shaped by our struggle for a socialist culture. It is in the socialist struggle of this world at this time that we recognize the transcendent.

Human redemption is an historical phenomenon, as Marx conceived of it, but human redemption is *also* transhistorical. In the creation of a socialist culture, in reference to the possibilities of ultimate transcendence, we redeem ourselves as human beings on this earth. However, that redemption is never complete until redemption is realized unconditionally. Our labor is in this world, our human redemption is here, but our unconditional reconciliation with essential being is always beyond. The prophetic is the new being, beyond the divide of sacred and secular.

As Tillich considered the possibilities of religious socialism, he probed the elemental roots of both religion and socialism, hoping for the transformation of both. His concern with religion and socialism was thus much more than with how the workers could be won back to the church.[39] Nor was he attempting to lure the workers away from socialist parties, although others might use a Christian socialism for just such a purpose. Rather, Tillich was seeking a religious dimension for socialism. By uncovering the roots of socialism in its secular eschatology and its propheticism in a "self-sufficient world," he made socialists aware of the faith already present in the socialist vision and sought to transform the vision into the truly religious realm as well. An interpreter of this aspect of Tillich's project, John R. Strumme, observes that Tillich was bringing into awareness the common faith expressed in the prophetic-eschatological symbol of the kingdom of God. Strumme writes:

> His theological interpretation turns on this symbol. One might even say that the theological thrust of his religious socialism was to discover the concrete social and political meaning of the prayer, "Thy Kingdom come." The kingdom comes in history, yet remains transcendent; the kingdom is "at hand," but it cannot be possessed. Its character is paradoxical: the transcendent is not in an undialectical opposition to history, but shows its genuine transcendence by breaking into history, shattering and changing it.[40]

The union of the socialist expectation with the sacred propheticism of the Judeo-Christian heritage is the aim of religious socialism.

With its roots in the universal demand, socialism has historically had the power to move the proletariat particularly. It has made the proletariat self-conscious of its destiny. "For in the universal tendency of socialism," writes Tillich, "is expressed the will of the proletariat to move beyond itself—not in the sense of an upward mobility into the bourgeois class, but in the sense of a new form of human being and of society as a whole."[41] Through the desire for and expectation of the classless society, the proletariat has placed itself in historical contexts that surpass its particular form of being. Socialism neither stands as a general demand over history nor represents a special empirical case. Socialism (or better, the socialist principle) is a particular principle that nonetheless expresses human being in general—an expectation of the new. This is its universality, its reaching back to the origins of life. It is not an intellectual, utopian socialism, as Tillich adds, but is based instead on the inseparable connection between the univeral socialist principle and the concrete struggles of the proletariat.

However, in the working class struggles against the oppression of the developing capitalist mode of production, and in the socialists' adoption of the scientific method also favored by the enlightened bourgeoise, socialism has become a substitute for religion. Rather than critically understand science, socialism has for the most part come to reject whatever contrasts with the rationality of science. Socialism, in other words, has come to place its faith in the empiricism of science. Not only is transcendence limited to this world, but living and meaning within this world are restricted to the techniques available to science. This, as Tillich warns, is a violation of the true socialist principle.[42] Socialism must recover the faith of the religiously unconditional. A science that critically examines the world is not in opposition to a religious faith in the transcendent kingdom. A religious socialism is placed firmly in both realms.

The socialist principle will continue to incorporate both prophetic and rational expectations. Moreover, "the tension between the prophetic and the rational elements in socialism is not a contradiction, but rather a genuine expression of a living expectation; it is that which constitutes its essence."[43] Our expectation is always transcendent and at the same time immanent. The prophetic goes beyond the known to a new creation, yet the rationality of expectation remains within the dimension of the knowable. Tillich thus states that expectation "looks for something 'other,' but not 'wholly other,' since that which is coming stands in direct continuity with what is present now."[44] The final expectation is for a transformation of human nature and, ultimately, the revelation of the kingdom of God.

Socialism theologically considered, then, looks beyond itself and its own achievement of a new social order. Tillich, near the conclusion of his discussion of religious socialism, makes clear that "socialism is not the end of socialism's striving," that the principle of socialism goes beyond concrete socialist forms in the creation of new being.[45] Marx would agree with this, and did in his own terms, but for Tillich this also means a movement beyond the secular future of human being to the transcendent being. The immanent expectation of socialism and the prophetic vision of the Judeo-Christian tradition are thus joined initially and finally. The path for us in our own time is through religious socialism.

As religious socialists our task is to relate the transcendent to everyday struggles of existence. God is that which is in us in the struggle for a humane world. Without the struggle, we do not know the transcendent, and without the transcendent, the struggle has no essence beyond itself. In religious socialism, we get rid of the false ideology which sees the transcendent as first existing in itself and then later enjoining its imperative. "The false ontology," the German theologian Dorothee Soelle writes, "allows us to idolize God-in-himself, God-as-such, so that justice is not the true essence, but an attribute among others."[46] There is no self-revelation of God other than through us in our historical struggle. Rather than being found in our full devotion to personal salvation, God is found through praxis in the struggle for human justice. Our redemption is in the prophetic imperative of life in this world in relation to transcendent being.

The socialist struggle in our age is simultaneously a search for the divine and a struggle for justice in human society. In overcoming human alienation and oppression we come closer to knowing our true being. And in our true being we come truly to know our God. Capitalism—in its oppressions and alienating forms—has dulled the human spirit and all but killed the transcendent being. Our sin, as Tillich conceived it, is the separation and the estrangement from our essential being.[47] In the struggle for religious socialism we hope to recover our wholeness, to heal our estrangement from the source of our being. Our prophetic hope is that the kingdom of God is near. The union is in the reconciliation of our estranged existence with the essence that is holy.

THE GRACE OF PROVIDENCE

By the grace of God we seek and struggle for reconciliation with ultimate being. The transcendent being—the beginning and sustenance of all things, that which we call God—reaches out through history to all who are ready to receive. God reaches out to us with grace; we reach out to God with our faith. We are thus brought into harmony with the divine plan. Our finite life is in the historical moment; and while our ultimate destiny is in the transhistorical, our finite existence is lived in the presence and reality of God.

God, or "being-in-itself" as Tillich came to refer to theistic being, is both a transcendent and immanent eruption into everything finite—nature, history, and human life. Through the grace of God the human spirit is led to strive beyond its present limits. But, we are cautioned: "While the Kingdom of God may be realized momentarily in human history as the vertical dimension intersects the horizontal dimension, fulfillment is never complete. Life continues as a tragic-ironic existence in which the critical function must be practiced."[48]

The possibility of fulfilling the ultimate meaning of the unconditional in a particular situation is á matter of personal and collective struggle. The risk of faith, as Tillich called it, is based on the fact that the unconditional becomes an ultimate concern in a concrete embodiment. The manifestations of the risk of faith are many:

> It can appear in purified and rationalized mythological symbols like God as highest personal being, and like most of the other traditional theological concepts. It can appear in ritual and sacramental activities for the adherents of a priestly and authoritarian religion. It can appear in concrete formulas and a special behavior, expressing the ineffable, as it always occurs in living mysticism. It can appear in prophetic-political demands for social justice, if they are the ultimate concern of religious and secular movements. It can occur in the honesty and ultimate devotion of the servants of scientific truth.[49]

Yet the foundation is not risk: "the awareness of the unconditional element in ourselves and our world."[50]

Even in our doubt, the divine is present and directed toward the unconditional. The religious spirit may, in fact, be its most profound in doubt. Expressing the religious basis of doubt in the face of God's silence, Fredric Jameson writes that "it is made plain in theological literature from the very outset that faith is to be described essentially as the longing to have faith, that the nature of belief lies not so much in some apprehension of the presence of God as rather of his silence, his absence—in short, that there is basically no real difference between a believer and a non-believer in the first place." [51] To which Tillich would add: "The profoundest doubt could not undermine the presupposition of doubt, the awareness of something unconditional." [52] Life is ambiguous and the transcendent is fragmentary.

We accept in faith the grace of God's providence. While not believing in the authoritarian doctrine of predestination, which was the by-product of a rigid Calvinism, we are aware of a general involvement of the transcendent in our lives at all times. There is a trust in God, a being-in-itself, a transcendent power, that is in the universe. And through us and our struggles for a humane world the universe comes to know itself. Providence is the wisdom of God expressed through time.

The eternal breaks into history in all periods. The prophetic voice announces to us the possibilities of fulfillment at a special historical moment. The earthly forms and processes grounded in the judgment of the transcendent become filled with the import of the unconditional. Through the grace of providence, received in our faith, we become aware of the unconditional element in ourselves and in history. Reconciliation between our existence and our essence becomes possible. We begin to experience the revelation of God's kingdom.

NOTES

1. James Luther Adams, "Theology and Modern Culture: Paul Tillich," In *On Being Human Religiously: Selected Essays on Religion and Society*, ed. and intro. Max L. Stackhouse (Boston: Beacon Press, 1976), p. 253.
2. Ibid., pp. 253–254.
3. James Dombrowski, *The Early Days of Christian Socialism in America* (New York: Columbia University Press, 1936), pp. 25–26, 41.
4. Ibid., p. 26.
5. Paul Tillich, *Political Expectation* (New York: Harper & Row, 1971), pp. 95–96.
6. Erich Fromm, *The Art of Loving* (New York: Harper & Row, 1956), p. 88.
7. Adams, "Theology and Modern Culture: Paul Tillich," p. 235.
8. Ibid., p. 248.
9. Ibid., p. 229.
10. "Humanist Manifesto II," *The Humanist*, 33 (September/October), 1973, p. 5.
11. Ibid., p. 6.

12. Ibid.
13. See the discussion in Benton Johnson, "Sociological Theory and Religious Truth," *Sociological Analysis*, 38 (Winter, 1977), pp. 368–388. Also see Charles C. Lemert, "Social Structure and the Absent Center: An Alternative to New Sociologies of Religion," *Sociological Analysis*, 36 (Summer, 1975), pp. 95–107.
14. Paul Tillich, *Theology of Culture* (New York: Oxford University Press, 1959), p. 133.
15. Paul Tillich, *Morality and Beyond* (New York: Harper & Row, 1963), p. 14.
16. Ibid., p. 20.
17. See Glenn Graber, "The Metaethics of Paul Tillich," *Journal of Religious Ethics*, 1 (Fall, 1973), pp. 121–122.
18. Paul Tillich, *Systematic Theology*, vol. 3 (Chicago: University of Chicago Press, 1963), p. 272.
19. See Roger Garaudy, *From Anathema to Dialogue*, trans. Luke O'Neill (New York: Herder and Herder, 1966), p. 39. Also see Russell Bradner Norris, *God, Marx, and the Future: Dialogue with Rober Garaudy* (Philadelphia: Fortress Press, 1974), pp. 1–14.
20. Harvey Cox, "Foreword," in Ernst Bloch, *Man on His Own: Essays in the Philosophy of Religion* (New York: Herder and Herder, 1970), p. 13.
21. Norris, *God, Marx, and the Future*, p. 6, quoting Ernst Bloch.
22. See Rosemary Radford Ruether, *The Radical Kingdom: The Western Experience of Messianic Hope* (New York: Harper & Row, 1970), pp. 186–187.
23. Herbert Aptheker, "What May Man Really Hope For?" in Nicholas Piediscalzi and Robert G. Thobaben (eds.), *From Hope to Liberation: Towards a New Marxist-Christian Dialogue* (Philadelphia: Fortress Press, 1974), p. 31.
24. Ibid., p. 33. On Latin American developments in the theology of liberation, see José Míguez Bonino, *Doing Theology in a Revolutionary Situation* (Philadelphia: Fortress Press, 1975).
25. Thomas W. Ogletree, "What May Man Really Hope For?" in Piedescalzi and Thobaben (eds.), *From Hope to Liberation*, pp. 45–46.
26. Ibid., p. 51.
27. Herbert Aptheker, "Response," in Piediscalzi and Thobaben, *From Hope to Liberation*, p. 52.
28. Ibid.
29. Paul Tillich, *The Protestant Era* (Chicago: University of Chicago Press, 1948), p. 258.
30. See Norris, *God, Marx, and the Future*, pp. 27–29.
31. Herbert Aptheker, *The Urgency of the Marxist-Christian Dialogue* (New York: Harper & Row, 1970), p.60.
32. See Leszek Kolakowski, *Toward a Marxist Humanism: Essays on the Left Today*, trans. Jane Zielonko Peel (New York: Grove Press, 1968), especially pp. 9–37.
33. Ruether, *The Radical Kingdom*, pp. 199–200. Also José Míguez Bonino, *Christians and Marxists: The Mutual Challenge to Revolution* (Grand Rapids, Mich.: William B. Eerdmans Publishing Co., 1976), pp. 118–132; and Hans Küng, *On Being a Christian*, trans. Edward Quinn, (New York: Doubleday, 1976), pp. 25–56.
34. Norris, *God, Marx, and the Future*, p. 39.
35. Adams, "Socialist Humanism and Religion: Karl Marx," in *On Being Human Religiously*, p. 158.
36. Shepherd Bliss, "Latin America—Where the Dialogue Becomes Praxis," in Piediscalzi and Thobaben (eds.), *From Hope to Liberation*. p. 95.

37. Paul Tillich, *The Socialist Decision*, trans. Franklin Sherman (New York: Harper & Row, 1977).
38. Tillich, *The Theology of Culture*, p. 42.
39. See John R. Stumme, "Introduction," Tillich, *The Socialist Decision*, p. xiii.
40. Ibid., p. xx.
41. Tillich, *The Socialist Decision*, p. 63.
42. Ibid., especially pp. 80–82.
43. Ibid., p. 112.
44. Ibid., p. 110.
45. Ibid., p. 132.
46. Dorothee Soelle, review of *Marx and the Bible* by José Miranda, *Union Seminary Quarterly* Review, 32 (Fall, 1976), p. 51.
47. Tillich, *Theology of Culture*, p. 123.
48. Ronald Stone, "Tillich's Critical Use of Marx and Freud in the Social Context of the Frankfort School," *Union Seminary Quarterly Review*, 33 (Fall, 1977), p. 6.
49. Tillich, *Theology of Culture*, p. 28.
50. Ibid.
51. Fredric Jameson, *Marxism and Form: Twentieth-Century Dialectical Theories of Literature* (Princeton, N.J.: Princeton University Press, 1971), p. 117.
52. Tillich, *Thelogy of Culture*, p. 29.

Epilogue:
Prophetic Criticism as a Cultural Form in the Reconstruction of Social and Moral Order

When Amos the shepherd and dresser of sycamore trees appeared, seven hundred years before the birth of Christ, there was in the Northern Kingdom a wealth fostered by the dominion of Jeroboam II. Amos, from his home in Tekoa, a village southeast of Bethlehem in the Kingdom of Judah, was suddenly overwhelmed by the presence of God and called to be a prophet. Speaking of the wealth and splendor in the palaces, while at the same time the poor were afflicted and exploited, Amos the shepherd exclaimed: "Woe to those who are at ease in Zion, and to those who feel secure on the mountain of Samaria, the notable men of the first of the nations, to whom the house of Israel come!" (Amos 6:1).

> Woe to those who lie upon beds of ivory,
> And stretch themselves upon their couches,
> And eat lambs from the flock,
> And calves from the midst of the stall;
> Who sing idle songs to the sound of the harp,
> And like David invent for themselves instruments
> of music;
> Who drink wine in bowls,
> And anoint themselves with the finest oils,
> But are not grieved over the ruin of Joseph!
> (Amos 6:4–6).

The prophecy of God at first startles Amos. The voice of God is compared with the roar of a lion about to fall upon its prey.[1] Yet all except the prophet are deaf and complacent; there is the need to convey to the people what the voice proclaims. Amos hears that Israel can live only in seeking God (Amos 5:4, 14, 15): "For Thus says the Lord to the house of

Israel: Seek Me and live; . . . Seek good, and not evil, that you may live; . . . Hate evil, and love good, and establish justice in the gate.'' Amos' mission is to exhort and to persuade, to communicate the divine presence in history, and to move the children of God to remove the oppression from their lives. A prophecy that begins in doom concludes with a voice of hope and renewal. In prophecy the conditions of this world are understood in terms of the transhistorical. The prophet, in attending to an intimacy with the divine, can do no other than speak as a servant of time and the eternal.

> Surely the Lord God does nothing, / Without revealing His secret / To His servants the prophets. / The lion has roared; / Who will not fear? / The Lord God has spoken; / Who can but prophesy?''(Amos 3:7–8).

The roots of our contemporary world, in spite of extreme religious secularity, are firmly anchored in the Judeo-Christian apprehension of human existence and fulfillment. We have an image of our essential nature and the possibilities for our human existence. This essence, however, has become separated from the conditions of this world, contradicted by human existence. The cleavage between reality and essence can be overcome only by human action through the creative power of redemption. The modern historical consciousness, in other words, is derived from the historical thinking of the Judeo-Christian prophetic tradition. Through the dynamics of history we experience the meaning that both guides and transcends our history. History and the transhistorical—time and the eternal—support our human existence. James Luther Adams thus writes:

> History in all its spheres is the arena of salvation, the realm in which the demands of the unconditional are confronted. Salvation occurs in time and through community, in the overcoming of the demonic powers that pervert both personal and social life. It appears in those forms and structures that give a local habitation to justice and love and beauty. And it is the work of a gracious, affirming, healing power moving toward the fulfillment of being and meaning.[2]

The depth of meaning, interpreting what we know and what we do, is known through our participation in the struggles of history.

The fullest apprehension of reality is in the union of the conditions of time with the unconditional of the transcendent. Our lives are a praxis of an involvement in the concrete historical situation and a sense of the unconditional depth of being. We are thus in the grasp of a truly critical and formative power. "The unconditionality of prophetic criticism, combined with the timely resoluteness of formative will under grace, can alone bring the fulness or fulfillment of time, the *kairos*."[3] The unconditional is known in history through the action that is inspired by a criticism founded on the prophetic. A criticism of the contemporary condition that is without a sense of the unconditional depth of meaning is not truly critical. Prophetic criticism has the power and objective of restoring our wholeness, bringing about a new world of fulfillment, uniting existence and essence.

In our own time the world has been broken apart by the development of capitalism. Not only has existence become separated from an essential nature, but our minds and spirits have all but lost the ability to comprehend and move beyond the separation. Bourgeois thought, appropriate to a capitalist society, analytically broke the world apart for the purpose of examination and control.

> It created a mind separate from the body, and a self separate from society; it distinguished art from science; it fragmented the world and human experience, the better to know and master them. In consequence, it achieved new heights of organization and technological progress. But in the wake of that triumph followed the tragic alienation of human beings from nature, society, work, and even from themselves. This astonishing achievement of bourgeois thought has led to our present intellectual impasse and moral crisis.[4]

Seeing and living in the world whole again is the mission of a prophetic criticism that is materially and theologically joined in Marxism and Christianity.

We currently live in an era that tends to reject the claims of a religiously based prophetic criticism. In his study of the Hebrew prophets, Abraham J. Heschel notes that "owing to a bias against any experience that eludes scientific inquiry, the claim of the prophets to divine inspiration was, as we have seen, *a priori* rejected."[5] A scientific rationality that is entirely based on empirical observation of this world excludes the prophetic critique of our existential estrangement from material and spiritual essence. History and its concrete conditions, accordingly, are bound solely by time; there is little that would guide us beyond the mortality of our earthly selves. This also means that an evaluation and judgment of our current situation are bound by the particular historical consciousness that comprehends nothing beyond itself. Not only have we silenced God, but we have silenced ourselves before God and before our own history. But still remembering our religious heritage, we begin to recover the prophetic in our lives and in our understanding of history.

Prophetic criticism is in sharp contrast to the ethos of the contemporary scientific method. Prophecy has very little to do with predicting the specific events of the future. In comparison to scientific prediction, with its explicit emphasis on human manipulation and control, prophecy is a form of address that calls human beings to an awareness of their historical responsibility and challenges them to act in ways that will change the existing human condition. The prophets of the Old Testament sometimes used the rhetorical device of visions of the future, "but they used them to try to rouse the people of Israel out of slumber and into the wakefulness and responsibility required by God."[6] The prophets foretold doom, but only if the people refused to keep the promises they had exchanged with their image of God. Human fulfillment was found in the exercise of moral will in the struggle for an historical future. The pessimistic character of a deterministic and predictive science is overcome in the prophetic hope for a humane and spiritually filled existence.

As social critics we are working in the realm of a critical and prophetic theology. We are positioned in a long tradition of religious reflection, inspired by the prophetic spirit. Social criticism—prophetic criticism—interprets historical and contemporary events with the intention of revealing and proclaiming their deepest meaning. And that meaning is grounded ultimately in the unconditional being that is in the process of knowing itself. We discover what the kingdom of God means in the process of struggling for our personal and collective history.

To engage in prophetic criticism is to engage in a form of cultural production. Prophetic criticism is a social practice that involves the creation of a knowledge that has cultural meaning in the existing society. As in all creative cultural endeavors, prophetic criticism takes shape as human labor, as a human capability for transforming the material and spiritual world. The aesthetic of prophetic criticism goes beyond the limitations imposed by the conditions of capitalist production. Indeed, the purpose of prophetic criticism is to expose the conditions of capitalism and to furnish the possibilities for creating a new existence. In prophetic criticism we transcend current existence, returning with new light for the transformation of our culture.

In capitalist society, however, there is the innate tendency to turn creative work into alien labor. Work ceases to fulfill the human need for expression and communication; we no longer realize ourselves and our critical function through creative expression. Our lives as well as our cultural productions tend to become subverted and alienated when lived and practiced in capitalist society.[7] The creative nature of cultural production is negatively affected when the cultural worker is restrained by the inner need to produce according to the conditions of the capitalist mode of production.

The substance and form of all our productions, then, are expressions of the underlying structure of capitalism to the extent that production has become alienated under capitalism. Our cultural productions are thus mediated by capitalism.[8] The final products of our labor are filtered through a multiplicity of mediations among the economic mode of production, the social structure, and the consciousness by which the cultural worker perceives reality. Whether our cultural productions are critical and reflexive or merely reflections of capitalism is shaped by our ability to think dialectically and by our conscious involvement in the class struggle.

The creative aesthetic, nevertheless, differs from the dominant mode of understanding in capitalist society in that it consciously seeks to transcend the objective, material world in both theory and practice. Art as a way of seeing, feeling, and perceiving is prophetic in its form and content. Not only does it penetrate beneath the surfaces of social reality to the underlying structures, but it aspires to go beyond that reality in actual life. The prophetic in creative production suggests how the world could be. In prophetic criticism, we are made to see the possibilities of another existence. The task of prophetic criticism is to demonstrate how our lives are historically produced, how our lives could have been different, and how they still can be transformed.

The aesthetic form is prophetic, then, at least in the sense of a secular prophecy. In its relative autonomy, the aesthetic of artistic production is a protest against existing arrangements while it at the same time transcends them. As Herbert Marcuse observes, "art subverts the dominant consciousness, the ordinary experience." [9] The aesthetic of cultural creation allows us in form and substance to transcend the social determination of our work. The intrinsic purpose of prophetic criticism, especially, is the creation of another sensibility which defies the dominant social institutions and modes of thought and belief. Prophetic criticism—in its aesthetic—reveals the essence of reality and suggests the potential of our essential nature. The critical function of prophetic criticism is its contribution to the historical struggle for human liberation. However, prophetic criticism, in attending to the sacred, adds to the artistic aesthetic and goes beyond aesthetics as commonly practiced. Prophetic criticism is directed to questions of ultimate concern.

Before turning to prophetic criticism in particular, we might ask what is the nature of social criticism in general, as shared by prophetic criticism. Social criticism has the responsibility of raising the consciousness of all people. Rather than serve the interests of the dominant class in capitalist society, the critic asks the question, as did the American literary critic F. O. Matthiessen in quoting architect Louis Sullivan: "Are you using such gifts as you possess for or against the people?" [10] Scholarship is to be used as a means for the removal of oppression and as a guide for a better society. The responsibility of the critic is to provide an analysis that has the power of creating a new form of cultural experience.

The social critic is necessarily a rebel and revolutionary, an artist who is opposed to capitalist values and who bears the costs for thinking and acting the way he or she does. [11] Because cultural productions tend to be conditioned by the capitalist mode of production, the efforts of the critic must necessarily contradict the established forms and products. The aesthetic of social criticism propels the critic into a negation of the capitalist condition and the creation of another reality.

The social critic is likewise a social visionary. The special task of the social critic, as witnessed in a long succession of American writers and literary critics, is "to be the custodian of ultimate values, the cultural conscious of the larger society." [12] And in bearing the vision, the critic seeks to change the way we see the world and the way we act in it, involving a revolution and transformation in those values and structures that prevent the creation of a new society. Critical work thus begins as an act of perception, originating in a full participation in the times. As James Agree, author of the critical work *Let Us Now Praise Famous Men*, stated early in his critical writing, the indispensible obligation of the true artist (or anyone) is "to try, under whatever confusion of pressures, to understand and illuminate and conduct oneself in accordance with the truth, in so far as one experiences." [13] Our experience of life in capitalist society places us in a position to consider the alternatives.

It is only by acknowledging the complexities of experience, rather than seeking to escape from them, that the critic approaches truth. Reality can be transcended only through an immersion in the matter of the concrete experience. Matthiessen, in his *American Renaissance*, drew from the critical literature of Emerson, Hawthorne, Thoreau, Whitman, and Melville and called for a union "between art and other functions of the community, that there should be an organic union between labor and culture." [14] That form should follow function, that social and literary criticism should follow from and contribute to the realization of human potential is the objective of organic criticism. The artificial division between art and living—between criticism and life—is thus to be broken. It is the dialectical union and tension between reason and passion, record and response, observation and participation, and art and life that provides social criticism with its aesthetic. The social critic can be none other than a seeker and a seer in his or her identification with the prophet.

Social critics are creators in that through their activity, they arouse in the hearts and minds of people the hope and will to realize the future of essential being. The critic is able to express the social and spiritual needs of the age. The critic's aesthetic response is an affirmation of those human meanings and values which the dominant society has reduced or tried to exclude. [15] Social criticism is a protest against the forcing of contemporary experience into a reproduction of the capitalist system and the turning of all things (including human labor) into commodities. The social critic directs a protest against the way things are within the concrete social and historical condition. And, as Marcuse adds, the aesthetic form of the artist (for us, the social critic) results in a transformation of the conventional context, "achieved through a reshaping of language, perception, and understanding so that they reveal the essence of reality in its appearance."[16] Social criticism breaks the hegemony of the established reality and defines what is real.

Social criticism as a specific mode of social consciousness thus contributes to changing the consciousness of those who are struggling to transform their own history. In moving beyond the ordinary and the familiar, we attend to the ultimate. Through a new way of seeing the world, through the seeing of things as they really are, we find a new way of being. Through this basic Marxist aesthetic, this critical and creative effort, we are made aware of our historical situation; we are inspired to build socialism today and doubtless will be inspired to go beyond it tomorrow.[17] We move toward the ever-widening horizon of the future, engaged in revealing the ultimate meaning of our existence.

The prophetic voice brings to social criticism the unity of the temporal and the eternal, the secular and the sacred. A social criticism that does not consider the sacred meaning of our existence systematically excludes the full potential and essence of our being. Prophetic criticism, however, brings together the historical and the transhistorical, allowing us to truly understand the present meaning of our social and moral condition. Prophetic criticism—in a sensitivity to what the moment demands, rather than a foreknowledge of the future—takes place with an awareness of divine involvement in history.

A cultural form that has the objective of reconstructing the social and moral order necessarily draws from the fundamental character of our religious and intellectual experience: the prophetic. The prophetic that forms the basis of our social criticism has the embracing qualities of having a long tradition, of being radical, and of being comprehensive.[18] Prophecy is firmly rooted in the tradition of the Old Testament, furnishing the basic intellectual and spiritual tradition continuing to the present. Moreover, the prophet is the radical critic of the time and place, witnessing to the divine judgment. And the prophet speaks on behalf of all the people, discerning the signs of the coming kingdom of God. A cultural criticism founded on the prophetic is thus profound in its source and its purpose.

Our prophetic heritage perceives the driving force of history as being the struggle between justice and injustice. We the people—in a covenant with God—are responsible for the character of our lives and our society, for the pursuit of righteousness, justice, and mercy. The social and moral order is consequently rooted in the divine commandments; morality rests upon divine command and concern rather than on the relativity of reasonableness. We seek to realize God's concern and command, the essence of perfect justice and love. The prophetic presence is real: "God is a living entity, closer than one's hands and feet, not a philosophic or theological abstraction."[19]

The prophetic furnishes us with the perspective for understanding the world and for working to change it. Out of our understanding of the present social and moral order, with all of its problems and contradictions, we are prepared to work for the creation of a new society. The essential task of prophetic criticism is to disclose the present so that our future may be constructed, all in terms of an image of the union of the historical and the transcendent. We learn from the prophet, whose eye is directed to the contemporary scene, yet whose ear is inclined to God.[20] Through prophetic criticism we are reminded of the moral condition of the times and of our moral responsibility for changing that condition. Prophetic thinking and acting bring the world into divine focus.

The concrete form in which divine revelation takes place, as the theologian Karl Rahner indicates, varies historically and is conditioned by the historical context in which it occurs.[21] The prophetic element has taken many forms in the historical development of our world, but its presence has been continuous. In our secular age, prophetic criticism brings to us the prophetic element. In times that are less dark, divine prophecy will be manifest in a more religious form. We accept the prophetic in the form in which it comes to us. The mission remains the same:

> The good in every prophecy is ultimately shown if it awakens us to the gravity of decision in courageous faith, if it makes clear to us that the world is in a deplorable state (which we never like to admit), if it steels our patience and fortifies our faith that God has already triumphed, even if in this world we still have distress, if it fills us with confidence in the one Lord of the still secret future, if it brings us to prayer, to conversion of heart, and to faith that nothing shall separate us from the love of Christ.[22]

In faith, with the grace of prophecy, we struggle to build a better world.

Prophecy—and the extent to which it exists in prophetic criticism—proclaims the divine concern for justice. The idea and belief that "God is justice" means the divine support and guidance for such human matters as the demystification of conventional thought, humanization of work, democratization and socialization of the economy, and the elimination of oppression of all kinds.[23] Apparent material issues are thus conceived of in terms of the transcendent, adding the necessary element that is missing in a strictly materialist analysis. Prophetic criticism is as much theological as it is sociological. In fact, the dialectic of both types of analysis gives prophetic criticism its power as a critique and an understanding of justice and injustice in this world.

To the prophets of the Old Testament injustice (whether in the form of crime and corruption or the condition of the poor) is not merely an injury to the welfare of the people (which it certainly is), but is a threat to existence itself. Moral comprehension, in other words, is rooted in the depth of the divine. This is a sense of justice that goes far beyond our modern liberal and legal notions of justice. For the prophets, the worldly virtue of justice is founded on the understanding that oppression on earth is a humiliation of God. Righteousness is not just a value for the prophet, as Heschel observes, but "it is God's part of human life, God's stake in human history."[24] The relation between human life and the divine is at stake when injustice occurs. Prophetic criticism for us seeks such grounding in its concern for justice. Justice is more than a normative idea; it is charged with the transcendent power of the infinite and the eternal, with the essence of divine revelation.

For the prophets, justice is like a mighty stream, not merely a category or mechanical process. In contrast: "The moralists discuss, suggest, counsel; the prophets proclaim, demand, insist."[25] Prophetic justice is charged with the urgency of the divine presence in the world. "Let justice roll down like waters, / And righteousness like a mighty stream" (Amos 5:24). In Heschel's phrase, "What ought to be, shall be!"[26] Prophetic criticism has a similar sense of urgency and depth.

Justice—and its lack of fulfillment—is a condition of the whole people. An individual's act expresses the moral state of the many.

> Above all, the prophets remind us of the moral state of a people: Few are guilty, but all are responsible. If we admit that the individual is in some measure conditioned or affected by the spirit of society, an individual's crime discloses society's corruption. In a community not indifferent to suffering, uncompromisingly impatient with cruelty and falsehood, continually concerned for God and every man, crime would be infrequent rather than common.[27]

Prophecy is directed to the whole world as well as to the inner spirit of the individual. The purpose of prophecy—and I am arguing for prophetic criticism as well—is to revolutionize history. Divine compassion is expressed in our own time. The call is personal: "And what does the Lord require of you / But to do justice, and to love kindness, / And to walk humbly with your God?" (Micah 6:6–8). And we are all judged collectively in the presence of corruption and oppression: "From the heavens Thou didst utter judgment; / The earth feared and was still, / When God arose to establish judgment / To save all the oppressed of the earth" (Psalm 76:8–9).

It is the source of the prophet's experience that gives prophecy its certainty and its urgency. "The certainty of being inspired by God, of speaking in His name, of having been sent by Him to the people, is the basic and central fact of the prophet's consciousness."[28] The experience without a confidence in its source would otherwise diminish, if not negate, the prophetic consciousness. But the prophet is in an encounter—a communication—with the transcendent. The self is surrendered—

however momentarily—to the divine; consciousness is with another. From knowing God, rather than from an absolutely mysterious experience, divine inspiration comes to the prophet.

The prophet, in turn, conveys the demand and judgment to others. Prophecy becomes social as well as divine. While prophetic criticism necessarily lacks the *sui generis* quality of the Old Testament prophets, it is nevertheless aware of being subject to a transcendent intensity. Prophetic criticism, even in the most secular of times, is compelled to listen to the divine source of inspiration.

The prophetic, even today, is open to those who are concerned about ultimate matters. In listening and addressing ourselves to the dialectic of the temporal and the eternal, history and the divine, we are in contact with the most profound questions of our personal and collective being. We are not looking for a mystical vision but are ready to consider profoundly the meaning of our present condition and our future possibility. Our prophetic stance in this secular age attempts to recover some of the essential quality of the prophecy of a time when the sacred was realized more fully.

Prophetic criticism is a form of understanding that leads us to the human actions that move us to a world which is closer to our essential nature, a world that is constantly aware of the coming of God's kingdom. Prophetic criticism provides us with direction, giving us a hope that is both temporal and transcendent. The meaning of our history is revealed—made known to us—in our own time.

The phenomenon of prophecy is based on the recognition that being human is being in contact with divine guidance. The purpose of prophecy is to establish the right relationship between human beings and the transcendent. For God to reveal the word through prophecy is an act of grace, of seeking to do justice. Heschel thus writes that right and wrong are dimensions of world history, not merely modes of conduct: "The existence of the world is contingent upon right and wrong, and its secret is God's involvement in history." [29]

The world—and its historical development—is the domain with which the prophets are occupied. "They are moved by a responsibility for society, by a sensitivity to what the moment demands." [30] The prophets remind us that God is not neutral and is never beyond good and evil. The divine is always partial to justice—uniting the historical and the eternal. Through the prophetic we maintain our contact with the divine in history.

This is the most precious insight: "to sense God's participation in existence; to experience oneself as a divine secret." [31] The theme of prophetic theology (and of a prophetic criticism) is God's concern for human life and our relevance to God. What we do with the divine presence in the world and concern for the world is the object of prophetic religion. In sharing divine concern we enter into the essential relationship with the transcendent in history. We are open to the living God. In the words of the fourteenth century hymn, "The God of Abram Praise," set to a Hebrew melody:

Praise to the Living God;
All praised be His Name;
Who was, and is, and is to be,
And still the same.[32]

But we have become separated from the essential relation of the human and the divine in the modern period of our history. A vast gulf now exists between our human finitude and eternal being. We have come to the point where the gulf is hardly recognized. The prophetic experience of apprehending the transcendent, and of realizing our being experienced by the divine, is all but a memory. In a reawakening, however, we are beginning to sense once again the divine presence in the universe and in our history. Through the prophetic spirit we are discovering ourselves as being apprehended by that which is beyond our selves—by the divine presence. Once again we are becoming known to our God. We are becoming capable of loving that which is beyond ourselves.

When we look back over the recent past, particularly in the United States, we are struck not by a progressive development but by decay and corruption. Puritanism itself—shaped by the demands of developing capitalism—has ceased to provide the source for recreating our essential being. Our inability to retain the prophetic wisdom that we live both in time as well as out of it, that there is a constant interaction between time and eternity, constitutes the dimensions of our modern tragedy. Prophetic writers in the middle of the last century recognized the impending condition. Nathaniel Hawthorne—still retaining a hold on the central Christian elements—was aware of the human capacity to transcend the self in the effort to realize perfection, a perfection that nevertheless remains beyond our grasp because of the limitation of our finitude.[33] The loss of this awareness is the condition of the protagonists in Hawthorne's writings and in other prophetic writings. In our secular age the human being has become his and her own messiah. What has been lost is the divine sense of pathos in which the human being can find completion only in something greater than the self—in a communion with and humility before God.

It is with Herman Melville's Captain Ahab, in *Moby Dick*, that the problem of the God-less individual is still most precisely portrayed in our prophetic literature. Ahab as the "man-God, the self-appointed Messiah" takes upon himself all the prerogatives usually reserved for God alone.[34] In assuming the divine role as a human being, Ahab, in all his self-righteous hatred of evil, becomes the incarnation of the evil he would destroy. Melville created in Ahab's tragedy the symbol of the self-enclosed individual who has increasingly brought disaster upon our society in the further development of capitalism with its associated religious secularity. The fate of Ahab is prophetic of the modern character.

Captain Ahab prophetically represents the modern individual who has charged the self with the task of finding redemption in this world only. Solely through the pursuit of material endeavors, the captain comes into the world to kill the white whale. Salvation for him is entirely in this world, on individualistic terms only. There is to be no collective salvation, no social solidarity, and no humility before God.[35] The modern Promethean individual has isolated the infinite within the life of the single, finite individual. Ahab—as the self-sufficient, capitalistic, antireligious individual—remains alive in our day. Should that the prophecy turn us once again to the proper relation betweeen being human and being known to God.

The prophetic imagination, then, reflects the presence of the divine in history. Things of this world have their meaning not so much in themselves as in the spiritual, in the word of God revealed in the world. The prophet and the poet (as for example Walt Whitman) are inspired to see the world in moments of divine illumination: "If the spiritual is not behind the material, to what purpose is the material?"[36] The material world is apprehended spiritually. Religious symbolism, as in John Milton's prophetic piety, becomes the eye through which reality is seen and understood.[37] The word of God is revealed prophetically in the matter of our history. The struggle for a good society is found in our concern for, and our awareness of the divine concern for, the kingdom of God.

In an awareness of the prophetic the essential relation between truth and reality is regained. The world—the temporal—is reality, and the kingdom of God is the truth. Thus Jacques Ellul, the French Protestant-scholar, writes that "the real provides the truth with the means for expressing itself, the truth transfigures the real by giving it a meaning that it obviously does not have in itself."[38] The truth of God's kingdom lies hidden in the present reality to be discovered in prophetic inspiration. History has meaning in the transcendent vision of the prophetic. The truth is known prophetically in the interrelation of the temporal and the eternal. The final judgment is in the end of historical time itself: "The judgment is clearly an end of history that results in a final work of re-creation, of the reinsertion of time in Eternity, of the destruction of death in order that there be Life.[39] In the meantime, until the end of time, our lives are lived historically and spiritually in the guiding grace of providence, made known to us through prophecy.

In the prophetic—and in the extent to which the prophetic is recovered in our own age in prophetic criticism—we discover the relationship between time and eternity. The events of this world are part of the larger design; truth is revealed in the reality of history. Our days are lived in the matter of this world *and* in the spirit of the eternal. Prophecy allows us to make the connection. Our historical struggle is thus for the creation of a social and moral order that prepares us for the ultimate of divine grace—the kingdom of God fulfilled. "Time is fulfilled in history, and history is fulfilled in the universal Kingdom of God, the Kingdom of justice and peace."[40]

Let us begin again to hear the word, to see the vision granted unto us. Eternal God, we can neither measure your height nor sketch your face, and yet we know that you are Creator.

NOTES

1. On the prophet Amos, see Abraham J. Heschel, *The Prophets*, vol. 1 (New York: Harper & Row, 1962), pp. 27–38.
2. James Luther Adams, "Theology and Modern Culture: Paul Tillich," *On Being Human Religiously* (Boston: Beacon Press, 1976), p. 248.
3. Ibid., p. 249. The reemergence of the prophetic in social action is discussed in José Miguez Bonino, "The Human and the System," *Theology Today*, 35 (April, 1978), pp. 14–24.
4. Warren I. Susman and Eugene D. Genovese, "A Note to Our Readers," *Marxist Perspectives*, 1 (Spring, 1978), p. 4.
5. Abraham J. Heschel, *The Prophets*, vol. 2 (New York: Harper & Row, 1962), p. 192
6. Harvey G. Cox, "Foreword," in Arend Theodoor van Leeuwen, *Prophecy in a Technocratic Era* (New York: Charles Scribner's Sons, 1968), p. 10.
7. Karl Marx, *The Grundrisse*, ed. David McLellan (New York: Harper & Row, 1971), pp. 132–143. In relation to artistic production, see Adolfo Sánchez Vázques, *Art and Society: Essays in Marxist Aesthetics*, trans. Maro Riofrancos (New York: Monthly Review Press, 1973), especially pp. 181–196.
8. Stanley Aronowitz, "Culture and Politics," *Politics and Society*, 6 (no. 3, 1976), pp. 347–376. Also see Stefan Morawski, "Introduction" in Karl Marx and Frederick Engels, *On Literature and Art*, eds. Lee Baxandall and Stefan Morawski (New York International General, 1973), pp. 3–47; Raymond Williams, *Marxism and Literature* (New York: Oxford University Press, 1977), pp. 206–212; and Terry Eagleton, *Marxism and Literary Criticism* (Berkeley: University of California Press, 1976), pp. 59–76.
9. Herbert Marcuse, *The Aesthetic Dimension: Toward a Critique of Marxist Aesthetics* (Boston: Beacon Press, 1978), p. ix.
10. F. O. Matthiessen, *American Renaissance: Art and Expression in the Age of Emerson and Whitman* (New York: Oxford University Press, 1941), p. xvi, quoting Louis Sullivan.
11. Morawski, "Introduction," in Marx and Engels, *On Literature and Art*, p. 26.
12. Richard H. Pells, *Radical Visions and American Dreams: Culture and Social Thought in the Depression Years* (New York: Harper & Row, 1973), p. 192.
13. Victor A. Kramer, *James Agee* (Boston: Twayne Publishers, 1975), p. i, quoting James Agee. Also see Alfred T. Barson, *A Way of Seeing: A Critical Study of James Agee* (Amherst: University of Massachusetts, 1972).
14. Matthiessen, *American Renaissance*, pp. xiv–xv.
15. Williams, *Marxism and Literature*, p. 151.
16. Marcuse, *The Aesthetic Dimension*, p. 8.

17. Heneri Arvon, *Marxist Esthetics*, trans. Helen R. Lane (Ithaca, N.Y.: Cornell University Press, 1973), p. 82.
18. These three qualities are presented in Leeuwen, *Prophecy in a Technocratic Era*, pp. 36–37.
19. Edgar R. Magnin, "The Voice of Prophecy in This Satellite Age," in Harry M. Orlinsky (ed.), *Interpreting the Prophetic Tradition* (Cincinnati: Hebrew Union College Press, 1969), p. 108.
20. Heschel, *The Prophets*, vol. 1, p. 21.
21. Karl Rahner, *Visions and Prophecies* (London: Burns & Oates, 1963), p. 15.
22. Ibid., p. 106
23. See Dorothee Soelle's review essay of *Marx and the Bible* by José Miranda, in the *Union Seminary Quarterly Review*, 32 (Fall, 1976), pp. 49–53.
24. Heschel, vol. 1, p. 198.
25. Ibid., p. 215.
26. Ibid., p. 213.
27. Ibid., p. 16.
28. Heschel, vol. 2, p. 206. Also see pp. 207–226.
29. Ibid., vol. 1, p. 215.
30. Ibid., pp. 218–219.
31. Ibid., vol. 2, p. 262.
32. From the hymnal of the First Baptist Church in America, Providence, R.I., *The New Church Hymnal*, ed. H. Augustine Smith (New York: D. Appleton-Century, 1937), p. 70. I want to acknowledge my debt and gratitude to Rev. Richard D. Bausman, minister of the church, for divine inspiration and guidance, and for his friendship.
33. See Giles B. Gunn, *F. O. Matthiessen: The Critical Imagination* (Seattle: University of Washington Press, 1975), especially pp. 107–123.
34. Matthiessen, *American Renaissance*, pp. 458–459.
35. See Carlos Fuentes, "Prometheus Unbound," in Lee Baxandall (ed.), *Radical Perspectives in the Arts* (Baltimore, Md.: Penguin Books, 1972), pp. 142–158.
36. Matthiessen, *American Renaissance*, p. 525, quoting Walt Whitman.
37. See Christopher Hill, *Milton and the English Revolution* (New York: Viking Press, 1977), especially pp. 233–237.
38. Jacques Ellul, *Apocalypse: The Book of Revelation*, trans. George W. Schreiner (New York: Seabury Press, 1977), p. 17.
39. Ibid., p. 173.
40. Paul Tillich, *Theology of Culture* (New York: Oxford University Press, 1959), p. 37.

Index

Peace, Nancy, 40
Pells, Richard H., 115
Piety, Augustinian, 57, 59–60, 63
Predestination, 24, 27
Prophecy, x, 1, 102–105, 108–114
Protestant Ethic and the Spirit of Capitalism, The, 27
Protestantism, 24–25, 26–33, 55, 60, 68, 73, 87
Puritans, 19–41, 42–43, 68; Great Awakening and, 56–60; religious and economic life of, 23–26; secularism and, 52–55; Roger Williams and, 33–39

Rahner, Karl, 109, 115
Rationalism, 7, 32, 43, 45, 54, 96
Rauschenbusch, Walter, 69, 82
Reformation, Protestant, 27
Religion: civil, 72–77; critique of, 6–7; evangelical, 44; Great Awakening and, 56–61; morality as basis of, 86–89; Puritanism in, 19–41; response to capitalism of, 67–72; secularization of, 42–63; 75; socialism and, 8–13, 95–98; spirit of capitalism and, 26–33. *See also* Theology
Religion and the Rise of Capitalism, 31
Revelation, Book of, 21–23
Rhode Island, 34–38, 50
Richardson, Herbert, 75, 83
Richey, Russell E., 83
Robertson, H. M., 28, 40
Robinson, John A. T., 83
Romans, 21
Rozwenc, Edwin C., 40, 62
Ruether, Rosemary R., 82, 83, 100

Samuelsson, Kurt, 26–28, 30–31, 40
Schleiermacher, Friedrich, 46
Secularism, 29, 30–31, 37; advanced, 65–67; beyond, 78–80; capitalist development and, 42–63
Siebert, Rudolf J., 17
Small, Albion, 70
Smith, Page, 39, 61, 63
Social gospel movement, 68–70
Socialism, 2–3, 43, 77; Christian, 65, 68–72, 90–91; religious, 8–13, 65, 87, 95–98; secular, 11–12; theological considerations of, 85–89

Socialist Decision, The, 1
Society of Christian Socialism, 71
Soelle, Dorothee, 17, 101, 115
Species-being, 2
Stoddard, Solomon, 57
Strikes, 51, 69
Strumme, John R., 96, 101
Sullivan Louis, 106, 115
Susman, Warren I., 114
Sweezy, Paul M., 62
Symbolism, religious, 12, 95

Tawney, R. H., 31, 40
Theology: of culture, 13–15, 38; Marxism and, 5–8; New England, 58–59; prophetic, 81, 102–115; secular, and beyond, 78–80; socialist culture and, 85–99
Thomas Aquinas, St., 30
Tillich, Paul, ix, 1, 3–5, 8, 11–18, 19, 46, 82, 84–86, 89, 92, 95–99, 100, 101, 115
Tocqueville, Alexis de, 74
Transcendentalism, 60
Tuveson, Ernest Lee, 39

Unemployment, 51, 66
Unitarian Church, 60
United States, 6, 48–61, 72–77
U. S. Constitution, 52

Viner, Jacob, 40
Void, sacred, 8

Ware, Norman, 62
Weber, Max, 26–32, 40
Welfare state, 66
White, Ronald C., Jr., 83
Whitefield, George, 57
Williams, J. Paul, 79, 83
Williams, Raymond, 39, 114
Williams, Roger, 1, 33–39, 54
Williams, William A., 62
Winthrop, John, 25–26, 33, 36
Woelfel, James W., 83
Wolin, Sheldon, 83
Working class, 7, 49–52, 64, 96
World War I, 51, 71
World War II, 51
Wright, Erik Olin, 62